the Love that Dare Not Speak its NAME

essays on queer desire and sexuality

Edited by Greg Wharton

The Love That Dare Not Speak Its Name
essays on queer desire and sexuality

BOHEME PRESS

Copyright © 2003 by Greg Wharton
Copyright © 2003 by The Contributors

All rights reserved. No part of this publication may be
reproduced or transmitted in any form or by any means, electronic or mechanical, including photocopying or any information storage and retrieval system
without a licence from Access Copyright, 1 Yonge Street, Suite 1900, Toronto,
Ontario, Canada, M5E 1E5

National Library of Canada Cataloguing in Publication Data

The love that dare not speak its name : essays on queer desire and
sexuality / Greg Wharton, ed.

ISBN 1-894498-07-0

1. Gays' writings, American. 2. Gays' writings, Canadian (English)
3. Gay men--Literary collections. I. Wharton, Greg, 1962—

PS509.H57L68 2003   814.8'09206642   C2003-902515-2

"A Sea of Decaying Kisses" © 2001 by Justin Chin, first appeared in *Burden of
Ashes* (Alyson Publications), reprinted with permission of the author;
"Trannyfags Unzipped" © 2001 by Patrick Califia, first appeared in *Unzipped*
magazine, reprinted with permission of the author; "The Sluts of San
Francisco" © 2002 by Simon Sheppard, a different version appeared in the *San
Francisco Bay Guardian*, reprinted with permission of the author; "Visibility" ©
2002 by Michael V. Smith, a different version appeared in *Cruising #3*, reprinted
with permission of the author.

Boheme Press gratefully acknowledges the Canada Council for the Arts for its
support of our publishing program.

Boheme Press
6 Lamont Creek Drive, Wasaga Beach, Ontario, L0L 2P0

To Ian, my lover,
and partner in thoughts
and so many other crimes against nature.

January 1893, Babbacombe Cliff

My Own Boy,

Your sonnet is quite lovely, and it is a marvel that those red-roseleaf lips of yours should be made no less for the madness of music and song than for the madness of kissing. Your slim gilt soul walks between passion and poetry. I know Hyacinthus, whom Apollo loved so madly, was you in Greek days. Why are you alone in London, and when do you go to Salisbury? Do go there to cool your hands in the grey twilight of Gothic things, and come here whenever you like. It is a lovely place and lacks only you; but go to Salisbury first.

Always, with undying love,
Yours, Oscar

— letter from Oscar Wilde to Lord Alfred Douglas

'Sweet youth,
Tell me why, sad and sighing, thou dost rove
These pleasent realms? I pray thee speak me sooth
What is thy name?' He said, 'My name is Love.'
Then straight the first did turn himself to me
And cried, 'He lieth, for his name is Shame,
But I am Love, and I was wont to be
Alone in this fair garden, till he came
Unasked by night; I am true Love, I fill
The hearts of boy and girl with mutual flame.'
Then sighing, said the other, 'Have thy will,
I am the love that dare not speak its name.'

— from the poem 'Two Loves,' by Lord Alfred Douglas, printed in Issue 84 of *The Chameleon*: *A Bazaar of Dangerous and Smiling Chances,* December 1894

Prosecutor:

What is "the love that dare not speak its name"?

Wilde:

"The love that dare not speak its name" in this century is such a great affection of an elder for a younger man as there was between David and Jonathan, such as Plato made the very basis of his philosophy, and such as you find in the sonnets of Michelangelo and Shakespeare. It is that deep, spiritual affection that is as pure as it is perfect. It dictates and pervades great works of art like those of Shakespeare and Michelangelo, and those two letters of mine, such as they are. It is in this century misunderstood, so much misunderstood that it may be described as the "love that dare not speak its name," and on account of it I am placed where I am now. It is beautiful, it is fine, it is the noblest form of affection. There is nothing unnatural about it. It is intellectual, and it repeatedly exists between an elder and a younger man, when the elder man has intellect, and the younger man has all the joy, hope and glamour of life before him. That it should be so the world does not understand. The world mocks at it and sometimes puts one in the pillory for it.

— Excerpt from the transcript of the criminal trial of Oscar Wilde, 1895

— CONTENTS —

Foreword: Daring to Speak / 10

GREG WHARTON

Why I'm / 15

ANDY QUAN

There is No Because: Some Thoughts on Interracial Dating / 25

MARSHALL MOORE

Not Something Tangible / 37

SKY GILBERT

The Etiology and Lost Art of "The Quickie" / 44

FELICE PICANO

(very) Trying Monogamy / 54

ROYSTON TESTER

Visibility / 67

MICHAEL V. SMITH

Confessions / 72

EMANUEL XAVIER

Seals / 78

MATT BERNSTEIN SYCAMORE

Trannyfags Unzipped / 93

PATRICK CALIFIA

The Sluts of San Francisco / 99

SIMON SHEPPARD

In Difference / 106

FRANCISCO IBÁÑEZ-CARRASCO

My Life as a Girl / 116

MICHAEL ROWE

A Sea of Decaying Kisses / 139

JUSTIN CHIN

Contributors / 150

Foreword: Daring to Speak

GREG WHARTON

At the height of the late-Victorian British Empire, Oscar Wilde's brilliant writing challenged smugness and prejudice and took on the establishment with amazing wit. Brave man. He also challenged the establishment by being seen in public with young "rent boys." Very brave man. But you can only push so much. Society—and the father of his lover Lord Alfred Douglas—got its revenge. In 1895, a London jury found Oscar Wilde guilty of violating Section 11 of the Criminal Law Amendment Act. (Prior to 1885, indecent assaults on persons over the age of thirteen were not punishable. Section 11 of the Criminal Law Amendment Act of 1885 revised the age of consent for girls from thirteen to sixteen. Lawmakers sought to make any indecent assault punishable by proposing an amendment that would make "gross indecencies"—regardless of the age of the victim—punishable as a misdemeanor. The chosen vague wordage was later interpreted more broadly than its intended purpose to apply to consensual same-sex acts between adults.) For his crime, Oscar Wilde spent two years at hard labor in prison.

It seems the more things change, the more they stay the same. Private consensual acts between adults, including same-sex sodomy, were decriminalized in England in 1967. But over a hundred years have passed since his trials and Oscar Wilde has still not been pardoned for his "gross indecencies" despite repeated protests for the Crown to do so.

In this new century, the struggle of LGBTIQ (lesbian, gay, bisexual, transgendered, intersexed and queer) people for full equality has become one of the most important and galvanizing civil rights movements. Yet with all the many advances that have been made, LGBTIQ people continue to face discrimination and death around the world.

In Canada, Customs officials regularly seize, detain or ban books, the majority coming from the US. Most of the books affected are written for, or published by, those interested in feminist, New Age, environmental or LGBTIQ issues. Not only are these seizures, detentions, and bannings seriously preventing the access of minorities to material directed to them, but they also discourage anyone who wishes to explore these viewpoints. Little Sister's Book & Art Emporium, located in Vancouver, British Columbia, has spent over half a million dollars fighting Canadian Customs since 1986 when Canada Customs banned *The Advocate*, a gay news magazine, on the basis that it was obscene. From that time, Little Sister's Bookstore has been targeted for special scrutiny by Customs. Material written by award winning-authors such as Jane Rule, Pat (now Patrick) Califia, John Preston and Susie Bright have been seized, while the same material was imported by mainstream booksellers without difficulty.

In the US, no federal law prevents a person from being fired or refused a job on the basis of sexual orientation. This nation's largest employer — the US military — openly discriminates against gays and lesbians. Mothers and fathers still lose child custody simply because they are gay or lesbian. And gay people are still denied the right to marry in all states. (Not that all gay folks want to marry, as you will read here, but it should still be an option, yes?)

Yet some changes really are changes. Although the laws in the US and Canada are still neither just nor fully equal (often grossly uneven depending on local laws), the general public's awareness and acceptance — at least to some extent — has broadened in the last couple decades. Simon Sheppard notes in his essay "The Sluts of San Francisco": ". . . despite all the rear-guard backlash against sodomy, the discourse around sexuality has broadened greatly over three decades. What was once unspeakable is now just more fodder for talk-shows. *Queer As Folk* is a hit. Sex, including gay sex and kinky sex, just won't shut up . . . ."

And that is where this anthology comes in. The focus is not so much of the title, *The Love That Dare Not Speak Its Name*, but the subtitle, *Essays on Queer Sexuality and Desire*. There are no essays with specific themes of politics, sexual laws, religious persecution, or the greater society's misguided mores. For that I suggest you start your education with Patrick Califia's seminal *Public Sex: The Culture of Radical Sex* (Cleis Press), now in its second edition.

The collected essays in *The Love That Dare Not Speak Its Name* speak freely and fervently on queer male sexuality. In thirteen insightful and thought-provoking essays, a diverse international group of bisexual, gay and transgender authors and essayists tell all about life, love, desire and sex: exploring how they perceive themselves sexually; how their sexual preference defines them; what turns them on; and how they like to get off. These essays are snapshots, individual glimpses into each man's life—brave and honest. Each essay is personal. Intimate. *Very* intimate. Several of the authors stressed to me how difficult their essays were to do. Emotionally draining. Even scary: confronting inner-demons, memories and fears. But they did it. And the results are inspiring.

I won't pretend to claim this book covers all aspects of gay male desire. That's not its purpose or intended focus. But it does do what hasn't been done often enough, if ever: give voice to a broad cross-section of queer men and their personal insights and opinions on desire. Written in numerous styles and voices, from the humorous (Felice Picano's "The Etiology and Lost Art of the Quickie") and biting (Patrick Califia's "Trannyfags Unzipped") to the raunchy (Simon Sheppard's "The Sluts of San Francisco") and graphic (Royston Tester's "(very) Trying Monogamy") to the poignant (Michael Rowe's "My Life as a Girl") and poetic (Justin Chin's "A Sea of Decaying Kisses") to the candid (Matt Bernstein Sycamore's "Seals") and confessional (Emanuel Xavier's "Confessions"), these essays nonetheless blend into an unforgettable and important chorus of queer men—not just the fabled Kinsey 6 gays of yesteryear (if there ever was, in fact, one such group) or the blond blue-eyed Ken-doll clones we so often see representing the LGBTIQ community in the media.

I'll even admit to playing God with the balance. I specifically chose these essayists (friends, acquaintances and respected peers) not just for their great talents and wordsmith savvy, but also for other, more personal and specific reasons: diversity. I truly did wish to include a broad spectrum—as broad as it *can be* for one book—of queer men speaking out about their sexuality, their desire, about the love they dare.

Once the authors were contacted and the themes discussed, the book took on a life of its own. The subject was there. The original idea was strong. But personal viewpoints, histories, lives, loves, desires and sexual escapades of the authors are what have made this collection truly alive. It is a fascinating read—whether as a broad study of queer male sexuality and desire, which is deserved and necessary—or as a before-bed pleasure. Either way, you're in for a treat.

Greg Wharton, editor
October 2002

The
Love
That
Dare
Not
Speak
Its
Name

Why I'm
ANDY QUAN

Why I'm attracted to redheads: For their reddity-red hair, in praise of readiness, to play connect the dots between their freckles, for the contrast between the colors of heat (glowing orange cinder-stick, crimson spark) and the water-colors of green and blue eyes.

Why I still don't make a lot of noise: I can't say that I discovered masturbation because I think I was always playing with myself. I'm surprised I didn't get whacked on the head or slapped on the wrist with a ruler. Maybe I'm more discreet than I realize. But when jerking-off became real, or at least messy and finite, I kept the door to my bedroom shut. With my parents' room down the hall, my pleasure was in the sweetest silence.

Why I hate small talk: Because I don't know. I really don't. I may have lots of reasons stored up over the years, and other theories. But live long enough and they all get disproven bit by bit.

I don't know why I'm not in a relationship.

I don't know why I've not had many.

Why I'm a fan of Tarzan: Because of that loincloth. Because of the names of the actors who played him. Lex Barker. Buster Keaton. Mike Henry. Because he was the sexiest thing on TV. Because I can still taste the summer Sunday afternoons, the blinds partly closed to stop the sun from robbing the images from the screen.

Mike Henry was my favorite. At each glimpse of him, my breath caught in my throat like a loaf of bread at the shapes of his muscles attached to every part of his body, the light dusting of dark hair across his chest, his abdomen. His straining thighs and calves as he clambered up a vine that hung straight down from somewhere just out of camera-range.

I wished to be at the top of that fake rope.

Why I'm a top: I've never managed to enjoy being a bottom. Certainly I'm jealous of those who can be both. Even the word is better, not a clipped top or mumbling bottom but the aerodynamic whispering projectile of versatile. It's a quality I strive for in other parts of my life.

I've met lots of guys who don't bottom ("the sad song of when two tops meet"). And I'm sure, almost 99.5% certain, that they don't get the following responses when they state their position: *"Really?" "I'm sure you'd love it." "C'mon, it will feel great." "Are you sure?"* It might be because I'm a smaller man and we like to believe a stereotype of big = top, small = bottom. And it might be because we've gone past that time in our history when it was expected that some guys are tops and others are bottoms.

But I'm sure it's because I'm Asian.

I'd be a much better bottom if the chip on my shoulder hadn't displaced up my butthole. If you look closely *(I love to be rimmed by the way),* it has faux Oriental writing on it, you know, the type where they make the strokes of the letters look like Chinese calligraphy. It says, "I hate being stereotyped."

Why I became a slut: It took a bit of practice, but I got there. Too many years of groping for romance and romantic groping and when I discovered gay saunas, I became graceful. I would get into conversations with men who I never would have met in my regular life. I could play at being confident. I learned disappointment, patience and happenstance. Later lessons were in one-night stands, cruising in parks and orgies: all good. Strange new worlds.

Why I'm politically incorrect: Even though I hate the phrase, the way it was stolen from us, and I long for the days we could tease our lesbian vegetarian friends ("lesbitarians") about whether they weren't being a bit too serious in wondering whether the people who'd harvested these sunflower seeds were unionized—even though I hate the phrase, it suits me. While I recognize that it's the heart that matters as well as kindness, a sharp mind, and some sort of intellectual-metaphysical-emotional attraction, it's ruled out in an instant reflex (reflux?). I try to blame chemical reactions, or at least my dick. But I fall stupid at the sight of a pretty muscle boy. Actually, they don't even have to be that pretty.

Why this works to my disadvantage: Because I'm not particularly muscular (though I've tried and *how do they do that anyways?*) and muscle boys gravitate towards each other and hang out in packs like wolves or lemmings or feral dogs even, and more often than not, the men who spend that much time on their bodies don't have too many interests and a fiction writer really doesn't give them a big hard-on. Though if they are smart and have a fabulous body too, it's even more obnoxious so I try to degrade them by stereotyping them as dumb steroidy beasts.

For some reason as well, in unusual proportions, when I click onto their profiles on any of the many find-a-dick/man/shag/mate internet sites, I find racist assholes (not the physical assholes which I quite like but more the imbecile species) who not only are looking only for other white men but say things like: *no Asians, no pretentious people, no geriatrics.*

Though I know I should feel solidarity with older men facing the same rampant too-fat too-old too-short too-not-white kind of same-discrimination: different-forms, or even build an alliance with pretentious people who are suffering from anti-pretentious societal tendencies, at the time I just feel pissed-off.

Why I'm lately amused: At big dance parties in Sydney, I've discovered a subset of pale gay men who are very muscular and like Asian men: they dance with or around groups of Asian men who fly down from Taiwan, Japan, Thailand, Singapore, Malaysia and other hotspots.

Unfortunately, most of these gay men being danced around are from another new subset of gay men at dance parties: the Asian muscle-boy, which leaves me bemused since I find myself finally the right color but not having gone to the gym quite enough.

Why I'm not bitter: Even though I can't always attract these tasty, white muscle-boys, the Asian muscle-boys don't seem to mind that I'm not as

THE LOVE THAT DARE NOT SPEAK ITS NAME

muscular as them. In fact: they kind of like me. I wonder whether this is because they were brought up in Asia and don't have this weird devaluation of Asianness that happens in places with a lot of white people. But I don't question it too much since they flirt with me, and I them, and on the dance floor (lasers, lights, music), it's good to rub my hands up and down over so many variations of gym-product, my Asian brother lovers, my lover brothers.

Why I feel bad: It does make me wonder, though, why I can pull Asian muscle-boys and not white muscle-boys. Is sexual racism as simple as that? Because Asians are Asian they're not as racist towards Asians. Surely not.

My shameful confession is that I champion the sexual attractiveness of Asian men (or basically any men that you've never considered before because you just think they're not your type, you've never been interested or it just isn't happening). And yet I have to admit that while I find other Asian guys attractive and have had sex with them, it never reaches fever pitch.

I had sex with the most beautiful Thai man in Bangkok's famous Babylon sauna. I kissed his exquisite jaw line, my hand on his smooth perfectly formed chest, and at the end thought, "If that doesn't do it, it's time to admit to yourself: you like (some) white boys the best."

Which is handy, I guess, since there's lots of them, at least in places where I've lived the last few years.

I know it's not a contradiction to like white boys and—like Asian boys too, but less—and to work towards gay men being less racist in bed. But it's not as neat a package as I'd like.

Why I like wrestling: It was the only thing on TV [except: see above—*Tarzan*]. It's way better than any static Calvin Klein ads or porno magazines. It's the body in motion, hyperactive overgrown children, arms swinging every which way, somersaulting, cartwheeling, reeling, falling, getting back up and doing it all again. The muscles move, strain and shimmer in the hot stadium lights.

Gay porn flicks display a limited range of movement (in/out, out/in).

Swimmers and runners are beautiful in their own mechanical way: stroke, stride, kick and dash. But it's not the same.

Gymnasts, now they're pretty good as well. Too many clothes, though.

Why I feel sad sometimes: Last year when I fell in love, maybe the most I ever have, and we settled month by month into a deeper relationship, there was this period near the end of the time that we were together when my physical attraction for my boyfriend waned. I didn't understand how it happened. I still saw the soulful brown eyes, his solid torso that amazed me, and his rippled back a mantle over it. But my work was heavy; I had some drama with family; and I was tired a lot of the time. I thought of sex, and seducing him, and finding a space in the day for it, but the other parts of life took over.

It was not that I lacked desire: a pot of sticky glue that was stirred and wanted release. We'd talked about our attractions to other men, and Tony wasn't the jealous type. That my head would turn on the street wasn't a problem. What felt wrong for me was that my extra-curricular lust got in the way of my normal sex life.

We watched porn videos a few times before bed. Tony would end up graciously making love to me. My head up near the ceiling above us, on the TV, somewhere else. The images didn't enhance our sex. They got in the way.

Months later when we'd broken up, I wondered if all my sexual freedom has tainted my ability to be with one person; if while I was playing the fields of sauna and stream, bar and street, fantasizing about my perfect knight, that in fact he was slipping further and further away from me.

Why I'm annoyed: Just now, I took a break from writing this to make a phone call. See, two weeks ago I went to a housewarming party with a friend, Antoine, and some friends of his I'd never met. They were ex-boyfriends, Ludo and Greg. They'd broken up a year ago but were best friends. I thought that both of them were attractive.

Ludo was the one I hit it off with, though. I found his face inspiringly handsome and the conversation flowed easily. I consumed many champagne cocktails. He went to meet friends for an all-nighter. I wasn't up for it, but told him to drop by in the morning if he wanted to. I know what it's like to want to cuddle up to someone after a big dance session, the party drugs slowly easing out of the system. He left, after taking my address and phone number. Not ten minutes later as I was returning from the bathroom, Greg dragged me into a bedroom, shut the door and tackled me onto the bed. His tongue in my mouth, I remembered that I was attracted to him too.

"You do know I just gave Ludo my phone number?"

"Yeah."

"And that I invited him to drop by in the morning."

"Oh, he's unreliable. He probably won't come by."

"And if he does? Do you guys do threesomes?"

"Not any more."

"So, if he comes by?"

"We'll go to my place instead."

Greg and I had a hot and drunken night.

The next week, we met up. I leaned into him for a tongue-kiss but was stopped.

"I just want to be friends."

Ludo didn't call me that week. He eventually sent an email saying he'd spoken with Greg and was a bit shocked by what happened. "He would recover" — a joke with a grain of truth and I could call him if I wanted to in the next few days.

I left it for longer than that. I didn't feel that Greg had acted in malice but he'd certainly managed to make me feel uncomfortable about contacting Ludo.

I called him just now.

He said a cheery, "hi" and not five minutes later, "I'm dating someone. I just thought I should tell you that. I met him last week." We maintained a conversation a little while longer before he said, "I don't think it's a good idea to see you now, but you never know. Sometimes these things last only a couple of weeks."

"You've got my number," I said, unconvinced, knowing that hooking up with two ex-boyfriends of each other was never a good idea; that I'd left calling Ludo too late; and that I didn't even know if I really wanted to get involved in something that became so complicated so rapidly.

That's why I'm annoyed.

Why I was a comic book fan: I can remember my first super-hero comic book. I was waiting for my father on an upper floor of an old, tall and thin building in Chinatown, the headquarters of our family association, one of the old clubs formed to provide support for the first Chinese immigrants. Membership was based on anyone with the same four last names. The tiny, shrunken, friendly woman who lived in the building had left me with a sugary drink and a comic book while she'd gone off to chat with Dad. I opened the worn and yellowing pages.

It told the story of a blind man, a lawyer, whose senses were so honed that he could fight, leap and throw his billy-club in all manners of ways to save people who needed it and battle menacing characters. His name was Matt; he had red hair. [See above — *redheads*.] When the corporate suit fell off, the change was miraculous: super-hero muscles bound by a skin-tight suit of the deepest red, an acrobat tumbling into my young, transfixed imagination, my obviously *gay* imaginings.

Many years later, I read articles in the gay press and chapters in books on gay subculture examining our obsession for the body beautiful. They posited that we have been over-influenced by a self-perpetuating ideal promoted in our newspapers and ads. Maybe with a broader range of images portrayed, our tastes would be more diverse.

Maybe.

But I remember that comic book and my initial attraction to it as something pure and simple, like the shine of the coin that appears under your pillow when you lose a tooth.

Why I can't understand other men sometimes: When we make love and they focus only on my cock (which admittedly I think is quite OK) or my ass (which I don't look at enough to pass judgment). The ones who aren't wild about kissing. The ones with a limited range of motion. They must think I'm crazy, licking them toe to head and dipping into each ear, and fingering each part of their bodies like a musical instrument: an ancient cello with a sonorous tone. I want sex with each part of their body, and in a dozen different rhythms.

THE LOVE THAT DARE NOT SPEAK ITS NAME

Maybe this is to make up for the fact that I'm vanilla. Exceptionally vanilla, with only a few sprinkles.

Why I don't mind bodybuilders: My friends, whom I consider much more down-to-earth and politically correct in their desires than I, are nearly uniform in their rejection of men who they consider too big. *Yuck. That's too much. C'mon, he has no neck.* While for me, they remind me of the comic books I read when I was young. [See above—*comic books*.] I want to dangle off of their over-blown chests like a rock-climber, feet swinging in empty air, hauling myself up, hand over hand, over the most difficult and impressive overhang.

Why I don't write about love: I'm scared. I meet men: friends and friends of friends. At bars and through sports teams and all the different ways you meet gay men. The ones I'm referring to are the ones who are alone, and have been alone all their lives, never serious dating, hardly a relationship, nothing much to say in that conversational domain. I consider my history, count up my two significant but short relationships. I think about all the types of love I have: for my friends, family and life. How little experience I have in love for a lover. I think about those men and wonder if I will be one of them.

Why I'm not sure about rimming: What's not to be sure of? That most vulnerable pink flesh: a perfect aureole, an invitation to go further and just as much, the sounds of pleasure from someone who likes being rimmed. If he's got a gorgeous ass, it's simply beauty surrounded by more beauty. It's like being offered dessert. Do you always have it? Or do you need to be in the mood for it? Or are you not really up for this particular slice on offer? However, when it's right, it's right. Who can resist? Not too sweet. Maybe a touch bitter even. As extravagant or basic as suits your fancy. Decadent. Dig in. Stick your spoon in it.

My problem is I tend to get parasites and an accompanying whopper of a stomach-ache. Which can set me in the mood of wondering what other unhygienic things I've been doing and pondering why I seem to get every single VD and bugaboo out there—Hep A, crabs, warts, unspecified infections of the urinary tract—small detours on the road to

ESSAYS ON QUEER DESIRE AND SEXUALITY

pleasure; trade-offs when I didn't know I was trading.

Why I'm confused: After all that I've said, I have met many men who I am attracted to who have good minds and hearts and forms. I do not compare them to the unrealistic men in my imagination. I try to be neither too needy nor aloof. I usually don't have to do much trying anyways, because when you click with someone, words flow easily and it's not difficult to be oneself. But I'm confused that I meet these men when I'm not available or when they're not available or that when they are, I can't turn it into something that is more solid than a couple of dates. Then back to my life as a single gay man.

Why I see a pattern: If you can see it *(dear reader)*, of course I can see it! It does, admittedly, seem a little pat. All this childhood fantasizing [see above]—am I stuck in a Peter Pan stage of arrested development?

I have an excuse.

I was protecting myself. What good would it have done to have crushes on other boys, or worse, a teacher? What about falling in love with your best friend? What about other people being able to see your desires out in the open so they can be shot down like in a carnival game? The prizes—the stuffed animals and cheap radios—went to the shooters, I knew that. Better to live in my head, a quiet room of strongmen and daredevils. No chance of getting caught then.

How helpful are fantasies? Or, not quite the opposite: are they not helpful? which is not quite the same as: how harmful are they?

Live them out.

We can see that this is happening. Men with leather fantasies can buy a harness, go to the local leather bar, or more extreme, book a dungeon through the local classifieds, pay someone to dominate or be dominated.

People of all proclivities can find an Internet newsgroup or chat room for any particular desire: sexual thrills from dressing up in large animal costumes, or from squashing things, say.

I went to the local gay wrestling club for nearly a year [see above—*wrestling*] and though the novelty and physicality exhilarated me, it was not in a sexual way. After months of wearing a costume of

23

THE LOVE THAT DARE NOT SPEAK ITS NAME

bruises on my forearms, biceps and thighs, after two neck injuries and a muscle torn in my shoulder, I decided to give it a rest. My fantasy was better in a form not so real.

What I really fantasize about is being in a loving, long-term relationship. How can I try that one out?

Why I celebrate: I have cared about many men. I have known good hearts. I have had sex with men who look like the ones I fantasized about before I ever had sex. I have had sex with men who look like anyone who I ever had a crush on. I have had sex with numerous men at the same time and it was fun. *Woohoo!* I celebrate sex both by doing it and by writing about it. I can write about my life believing that honesty is helpful, useful even, sometimes transgressive. I embarrass myself but don't flinch as much as you'd think.

I celebrate because it's good to be appreciative.

And because pushing borders can lead you to the most wonderful lands.

And because there's still time.

There Is No Because:
Some Thoughts on Interracial Dating
MARSHALL MOORE

Where relationships are concerned, white men are not my preference. If I were single, I wouldn't completely rule out the idea of a white boyfriend, and I've certainly had my share (plus two or three other people's shares) of one-night-stands with them, but they're not the ones who make my heart beat faster. I've been asked why any number of times in the fifteen years I've been a sexually active adult, and there's not just one answer. I can't boil it down to one or two sentences and don't really want to try. (I was raised by a pack of chattery Southern women and couldn't be succinct if I tried. Geography is destiny.)

To put this essay into perspective, I should explain a bit about myself. I'm a white guy in his early 30s. I was raised in a small, college town in eastern North Carolina, which is not the most progressive part of the country or even first runner-up. During my entire dating history, I've only gone out with a few white men for any length of time: one was a fair-complected Armenian, one was Jewish, and two were deaf. So much for the boy-next-door paradigm. The rest have been black, Latino or Asian. My partner, Anthony, is Vietnamese. I think that covers the need-to-know stuff. Having disclaimed, I'll get on with the show.

Attraction isn't a choice. I'm not convinced men choose what makes our dicks hard; we don't choose which sex we fall in love with. I'm careful saying this because it sounds like the "I can't help being gay, so please accept me" whine of previous decades' queer politics: I'm not interested in making apologies or offering justifications. However, I've never made a conscious decision to be attracted to men and not women. It was just there. Coming out was the decision to call my sexual orientation by its true name and act on it. Inasmuch as I made a choice, it was to live consistently with the way I'm made. A fine distinction, yes, but an important one. It follows that some men are more attractive to me than others.

For example, I'm into guys but not body hair. A little chest and leg hair is great (armpit hair is even better), but if I wanted to shag a furry beast I'd break into the zoo at night. A smooth-skinned partner is attractive to me in his own right, not to mention sexually practical for not requiring frequent breaks to pluck hairs off my tongue. Skin color and texture are factors too: I love the porcelain-olive shades of Asian skin and the rich tans and browns of black men and Latinos. I'm attracted to men shorter than I am (I'm 6'1, so that doesn't narrow the field by much), and slighter; I don't want to look up when I kiss someone. My ideal tends to be slender and wiry but not skeletal. I'm attracted to neither muscles nor fat.

At the risk of overlooking the forest for the trees, I'll admit I've fallen in love with details of various men. It's vulgar to reduce people to specific body parts—that's not far from the cock size stereotypes, or, I guess, for straight guys, tits—but the gods truly do reside in the details: my partner's skin, hairless, and elaborately tattooed; the shape of a Chinese ex's eyes; a black ex's dark, rich skin and firm, full butt; those luscious lips; someone else's cinnamon-tan skin; soft, curly Latin hair and that accent. Details, yes, not the whole person, but the sort of thing I can't help but appreciate. If, for example, a handsome white guy and a handsome non-white guy were walking down the street together, I know which one I'd look at first. When I'm changing clothes in the locker room at the gym, want to guess where my gaze goes? It's an atavistic reaction, below the level of conscious control. I'm aware of it now, so there's a conscious layer too, but the desire comes from the same place.

Affinity for certain cultural traits is a component of sexual attraction, too. One friend, a white man whose partner is black, said he feels non-white men have a different way of "being in the world." They're more aware of how they relate to other people, more conscious of their surroundings, more attentive to the nature of power in their relationships. A different perspective, from a white man whose partner is Chinese: "I like men who can control themselves." He is particularly attracted to the restraint, discipline and reserve he has observed in Asian cultures. A third said he appreciates men from cultures of respect, which is a trait white Americans tend to lack. Even white Europeans tend to be a more comfortable fit for him.

There is merit in all three perspectives. I'm reluctant to endorse

ESSAYS ON QUEER DESIRE AND SEXUALITY

blanket statements—for example, Asians born into Western cultures may not be as restrained as my friend's statement would suggest. Apart from physical appearance, they may not be so different from anyone else. The shape under the blanket statements is, I suspect, an attraction to difference: a different way of looking at the world, a different body shape or hair color or facial structure, skin of a different color contrasting handsomely with your own. Familiarity may be comforting, but I find difference more exciting, more attractive.

Being from the South, I grew up with an outsider-looking-in perspective on my identity as an American. Below the Mason-Dixon Line, adults interact (or used to) with a certain formality I haven't seen elsewhere in this country. There's the hospitality thing, which actually does exist outside of stereotype and legend. Southerners (white ones, at least) are more likely to open their homes than Americans-at-large who are generally only hospitable to people they know. When I've visited Asian and South American friends in their homes while travelling abroad, the inevitable warm reception has always come as a familiar surprise. The interactions I have with friends and lovers from overseas have often reminded me of the graciousness I experienced growing up where I did.

The South is one of the few places in the United States where a white man can grow up and not feel entirely American, while also being descended from the first people to migrate here. That may have changed in recent years as the media and the Internet have melted regional distinctions, but for a kid growing into self-awareness in the Seventies and Eighties, it was still true. The messages I'd gotten from TV shows and the news and even from history classes, about what it meant to be Southern:

> We had seceded and the rest of the country wasn't sure annexing us back had been the best idea;
> We were poor, backward, uneducated and probably inbred to boot;
> We were all racists.

I grew up with that uniquely Southern sense of prickly pride in my origins—due to a sense of inferiority to Midwesterners and Yankees, I'm sure, even if I'd have never admitted as much. Everyone from up North talked too loud in those god-awful accents, was rude, drove too fast and couldn't make a decent glass of iced tea.

27

THE LOVE THAT DARE NOT SPEAK ITS NAME

I'd never fly a Confederate flag but do I have reservations about the Stars and Stripes. Southerners have a long history of mistrust of the federal government: I've heard people say Washington's only roles should be to print money, deliver the mail and declare war. Yes, I'm American—I have the blue passport, the accent and the delusions of entitlement to prove it—but in the hierarchy of my identity—as defined by place—Uncle Sam comes second. As the bumper sticker says: *American by birth, Southern by the grace of God.*

My early experiences with race were very limited. North Carolina until the mid-1990s, when I moved to Washington, D.C., was a stifling hell rendered in black and white. There were very few Asians and Latinos. I had a couple of Korean friends growing up—their families had moved to Greenville, my hometown, because of the university. There was one Chinese kid in my junior high school. I think there were two Latina girls in that school: one hung out with the white kids and one hung out with the black kids. So much for diversity.

Gay relationships are to some degree about the phenomenon social scientists call *mirroring*—looking for parts of yourself in your partner. It makes sense that an in-country expatriate such as myself would have a worldview similar to that of a person of color. Is it such a leap from being gay and Southern in an increasingly mainstreamed America and being ethnic? Or from some other country? There's a difference, yes, but the divide is not a sociological Grand Canyon, either. Not if you've been paying attention. If you've forgotten your roots for a moment, speak with an accent and someone will always remind you where you're from.

Being gay confers a certain identity as well. Even if there's no single way to be gay, no monolithic culture, a certain guarded perspective becomes inevitable when you are the obvious faggot in grade school. I lived through the archetypal ostracism and abuse in the years before lawsuits were ever a possibility. I was beaten up and chosen last for teams. Kids on the bus would spit in my face and knock me down. My bike and locker were vandalized repeatedly. And so on. This went on for years and only ended when I transferred (escaped) to more progressive school in a different city.

I wasn't treated much better at home. My father, an ex-Marine from rural Louisiana, had definite ideas about how boys should act and I was-

ESSAYS ON QUEER DESIRE AND SEXUALITY

n't even coming close. As I recall, the physical abuse ended in my early teens. I believe I finally told him I was going to hit him back. Or possibly when I joined the swim team and had to wear a Speedo, the bruises on my legs and butt were too obvious. I don't know. He didn't deal with my pierced ears well a few years later, but at least he kept his hands off me. My mother's approach was more subtle: she often took the opportunity to say vicious things about gay men of her acquaintance—as if by drilling in how repulsive she found them, I'd take the hint and go straight. With this kind of thing going on, I got a loud and clear message: *You don't belong; you're not like us.*

I grew up assuming people could look at me and tell I was gay. As I've gotten older, I've left behind the queeny mannerisms and the loud clothes that blared BIG FAG. Being queer wasn't a phase but being blatant about it was. (In my own defense, I'm a product of the Eighties—not a decade memorable for its subtle fashions and hairstyles.) Now, almost twenty years later, I know I'm not that obvious. If you're gay, or at least reasonably perceptive, you'll be able to tell which team I bat for; otherwise, probably not.

Would the same kind of mistreatment have happened if I'd been born straight but kind of awkward? Would the scars have been as deep and long lasting? No. I firmly believe not. Awkwardness is a trait you can grow out of. Being gay isn't.

My skin is white but I have always carried the presumption of visible otherness—membership in a stigmatized group. I've occasionally had to fear for my safety. I've been attacked.

In some small way, *I get it.*

The first man I ever slept with—who ended up being my first boyfriend—was black. We were involved off and on (more off than on) for a year.

I'd gone to DC with friends for a weekend of clubbing. This would be my first time setting foot in a gay club. Before going out, I subdued my nervous stomach with beer and several Pepto-Bismol shots. Nothing happened my first night out, but the second night, in the bar formerly known as the Fraternity House, someone in the crowd grabbed my arm.

A black guy. Christ. This is not what I had in mind, I remember

29

THE LOVE THAT DARE NOT SPEAK ITS NAME

thinking.

Two of the guys I was with were deaf.

Help, I signed to them.

They laughed at me and disappeared into the crowd, leaving me to fend for myself.

The black guy won a few points by signing, *Are you deaf?*

No, I replied. *I'm hearing but my friends are deaf, and it's too loud in here to hear anything.*

He misunderstood me, thought I was saying I was deaf, and dragged me to a less crowded part of the bar to keep talking (signing). His ASL wasn't great—to be honest, mine wasn't much better then—but he seemed to be a nice guy, and in better lighting I noticed he was kind of cute.

"Stay here," he said, holding up a finger.

When he turned to grab paper and a pencil from the bar, I broke the silence: "I can hear you."

I felt guilty enough already, more so when I saw the stunned look on his face. It's not like I lied to him, I reminded myself. I told him I was hearing and he didn't understand all of it. I didn't want my initial reluctance to be about his race. I hoped it wasn't, and while we talked, I analyzed my feelings. What I came up with satisfied me—at first glance, he just didn't seem very attractive. Once we started talking, I found I liked his big Bambi eyes and his wiry build. He was handsome in an off-kilter way.

Eventually we got far enough past the indignation he was using to mask his lack of comprehension (he speaks four languages fluently and loathes being wrong; to this day, more than a decade later, he still insists he understood what I signed) for me to realize I was about to get laid. I offered him a ride home about the same time he was giving up on getting into my pants. That night, I practically raped him.

In the time we spent together, Scott pushed me: he thought I was a cute hick with a lot of potential. He had grown up in D.C., had lived in Europe, had expensive tastes, admitted to being a snob, and didn't have a problem with that. To my parents' credit, they hadn't brought me up to be a racist, per se. Several years before I met Scott, long before I was ready to identify publicly as gay, I'd quit going to family reunions: I was

ESSAYS ON QUEER DESIRE AND SEXUALITY

sick of hearing my great-uncles and aunts' tirades about *the niggers this, the niggers that, the niggers the other thing, and you can't drive in Miami any more because of all the damn Cubans in the streets.* Growing up in eastern North Carolina, I'd acquired a subtle sense of white supremacy via sheer osmosis. My relatives' casual racism turned my stomach and I rejected it in its overt forms, but until I met Scott, nothing had challenged my attitudes on their more subtle and intimate levels.

Scott single-handedly took a wrecking ball to most of my preconceptions. It's difficult to feel superior to someone who is successful, fiercely independent, well-dressed, articulate in twice as many languages as you yourself speak, who has lived overseas . . . in short, who is already the sort of person you want to be. And while we're on the subject of superiority, he had a closet full of Armani and Hugo Boss when I didn't even own a belt, much less know I was supposed to wear one that matched my shoes. Scott knew that's what he was doing, too, and reminded me every chance he got. One night with his brothers and sisters, after dinner, he put me on the spot:

"Haven't you learned something about black people, dating me? I mean, you didn't know much before, did you?"

All eyes were on me.

"Yeah. Black men aren't necessarily *bigger*."

They all screamed. I'd won that round. I usually didn't. When I was with Scott, I had to confront the fact I was over my head and out of my league.

To backtrack further, I think my first full-on high school crush was on a biracial Chinese-Caucasian guy, Sean Ng. I was in boarding school; he was a townie. I don't remember how we met. I liked him immediately. I was already sizing men up, even if I didn't recognize what I was doing and what it meant. At first I didn't think Sean was too cute—he had a weak chin. No matter. Weak chin or not, we were inseparable. Before long I figured out I was head over heels for him. I loved him and could say the words in my head, if not out loud. I kept hoping he would kiss me, but I was scared to initiate anything myself. Nothing ever did happen between us: in less than a year, the friendship dwindled away. I was inconsolable for months afterward. I've looked back and wondered whether some kind of imprinting happened because of Sean: just as

31

THE LOVE THAT DARE NOT SPEAK ITS NAME

newly-hatched ducklings follow around the first thing they see, thinking it's their mother, did my first high-school crush predispose me toward Asians? Perhaps. By extension, did these two relationships predispose me toward attraction to men of color? Perhaps.

There's an element of rebellion involved in dating outside my race, and the rebel in me (there's that Southerner again) loves it. Rebellion against what, or whom? Rebellion against society's racism? Or the racism I grew up with? Against specific people whose views I've come to find offensive? I don't have one single answer, but I don't see rebellion as a significant motivation so much as an after-the-fact benefit.

For me, coming out (in the sense of finally admitting it to myself and others) was the act of rebellion. Coming out was the act of recognizing all the disinformation I'd been given about myself all my life for what it was, and rejecting it. Being gay wasn't about being doomed to a life of lonely, furtive perversion with diseased strangers in public bathrooms; it was about the guy in my Latin class I had a crush on and wanted to make out with. It wasn't about me being a failure as a male, as my ex-Marine father seemed to believe. It wasn't about whether I satisfied or disappointed my parents; I only wanted room to be who I really was, without regard to what they thought, expected, dreaded or were trying to deny. It was about self-definition. Autonomy. The personal may be the political but at the age of 18 my worldview didn't extend too far beyond the end of my dick, and when I came out, I was fed up with the imposition of other people's definitions. I wiped the slate clean and, in so doing, made room to write on it in multicolored chalk. Even if I didn't know it at the time. That came later.

There's nothing inherently rebellious about having my tongue up some black guy's ass or indulging in a three-way with two Asians. Anyone who's thinking about it that much at the time is probably not paying attention to his partner or partners and might as well not be there. Whatever I do and whomever I do it with is about him (or them) and me at the time. Sociological analysis shouldn't take place before the come is toweled off: besides being tacky, racial politics before sex equals a weird kind of objectification.

Boiling this discussion down to just sex is a mistake as well. This is

ESSAYS ON QUEER DESIRE AND SEXUALITY

the same mistake many straight people make. Being gay is not merely a vehicle for obtaining a particular kind of sex. My partner and I are still gay even when we're not in bed. We're gay when we're doing dumb mundane domestic chores like folding laundry and cleaning the bathroom. In our case, a dyadic relationship works. The issue is still self-determination, not buttfucking and the ways to obtain it.

I don't approve of fetishizing men by race. Having been a blond-haired blue-eyed accessory before, I've had a taste of what objectification is like. It works two ways. White rice queens with their interchangeable and often much younger Asian boyfriends creep me out: what are their post-coital conversations like? Do they actually have anything to talk about? Obviously both parties are getting something out of the arrangement, and perhaps I'm naïve in my egalitarianism, but this approach doesn't work for me at all. I also get a little weirded out by the white guys who think the only good sex is the kind that involves being ravaged by a rough, uncut Latin *cholo* with his girlfriend's name tattooed on his neck, and the nelly white bottoms who only want to put out for black tops. It's one thing to be attracted to a certain look. Black dick, for example, is great, but if you're not interested in the men the dicks are attached to, then do yourself (and them) a favor and buy a lifelike dildo. This is just the flip-side of "I don't do chocolate." I always want to ask, *What's wrong with you? Why not?*

Another facet of multicolored love is the way I am perceived based on which race I am with. I confront this with some regularity and am equally amused and appalled by the comments I've heard when people have found out the race of someone I was dating or sleeping with.

Scott brought the point home not long after we met: "I'm sure when people see us together, they think I am the one penetrating you." He wouldn't elaborate on that, but it didn't take long to figure it out: as a very young, very slender, very blond and not very masculine white boy with a conservative-looking, older black boyfriend in a suit, I must be the one with my legs in the air. Whether it was true or not.

Everyone knows that:

> All Asians are passive bottoms, so if I'm dating one, then I
   must be a top;

33

THE LOVE THAT DARE NOT SPEAK ITS NAME

> White guys who date black guys are trashy bottoms;
> Black guys like it when white guys talk ghetto, especially in bed ("Fuck me with that nigger dick" is especially endearing);
> Latin guys are chronically dramatic, unfaithful Lotharios, so if I'm dating one, I should know what I'm getting myself into;
> Black men have the biggest dicks, followed by Latinos, with white guys somewhere in the middle, Asians generally very small and has anyone ever actually seen a Middle Eastern guy's penis?—size must have influenced my choice of a partner some how, and even if I say it didn't, I still shouldn't be offended by the fact you brought up the subject of my boyfriend's cock size.

When I told my sister I'd met Anthony and e-mailed her a picture, her response was a dry, "You sure do like Asians, don't you?"

I thanked her for her sensitivity and tact. "Nice of you to say, 'Congratulations, I'm happy to hear the good news.' "

"Well, you know how you like to travel around the world, sampling the local cuisine."

People are going to see a fetish where there isn't one, I've decided. Explaining I simply find someone of whatever race interesting, hit it off with him, appreciate a certain look but don't think it's the end-all-be-all—this will only get me so far. The psychology behind this eludes me. Maybe it makes life seem more exciting than it really is. Maybe people like the idea of all this exotic sex I must be having, and they want to live vicariously—orgasms by proxy, with people they themselves would never ever fuck. I don't know. The older I get, the stupider other people seem, especially where race is concerned.

When I asked friends and acquaintances about the attraction to dating men outside their own race, *self-loathing* came up several times. Interestingly, white men weren't the ones who tended to offer this as a reason. "I'm attracted to what I don't have," a Filipino friend said, rubbing the skin on his forearm to make a point. "I like light skin, green or blue eyes, blond hair, body hair." A black friend put it more bluntly: "I wouldn't want to date me." He once told me he'd picked up another black man out of curiosity, to see what the sex would be like. He wanted to know what he was like in bed from the point of view of the white guys

ESSAYS ON QUEER DESIRE AND SEXUALITY

he usually slept with.

"What was that like?" I asked him.

"Interesting."

Inasmuch as I've ever been motivated by self-loathing, it hasn't affected this part of my life. In my teens I decided to suppress my accent—I didn't like being picked on because of my Down East twang, and I'd begun to notice how society equated my accent with stupidity. (Even now, when the comedienne Margaret Cho wants to indicate someone is dumb, she affects a Southern drawl. We're one of the last groups it's not taboo to pick on in this manner.) I'm not repulsed by tall, blond white guys because they remind me of myself, and it's not that we have nothing in common. I've often joked that if I wanted to bonk the boy next door I only need to jack off. This hypothetical guy (*the boy next door* is always white, by the way) is just not as attractive as the Chinese (black, Filipino, Armenian, Mexican, whatever) guy across the street. In all honesty, I don't lack self-esteem. I used to, but somewhere along the way I acquired an ample supply. I have my issues, but self-hatred is not one of them.

In the space of one essay, you can't even scratch the surface; you can only point at it. It's downright excruciating to look for a blanket statement to explain why I would choose a person of color for a partner instead of a white man. To begin with, the concept of choice is funny: I meet who I meet, and either there's chemistry or there isn't. Plus, there's a fine line between stereotypes and individual realities. There's no one single reason *why*: it's *all of the above* and *none of the above* at the same time. Yes, people do have their preferences and their requirements, but there's no recipe for relationships; they're not so easy to break down into component parts. You always overlook something; you always oversimplify. Even choosing the right words can be daunting—there's that lingering concern about coming across as a total racist idiot, even if I know I'm not one. And this is one tiny part of a greater social issue: American history hardly lends itself to comfortable conversations on the subject of race.

Reading this essay, there are people who will call me a racist just for speaking candidly about my experiences. There are people who will look for reasons to say I'm a paragon of white arrogance and oppression, that I subjugate my boyfriend every time we make love or that I'm one of those strange white people who want to be some other race to make their lives seem more valid, or whatever. Let them.

I prefer to stand or fall on my own merits. When I meet a new Asian person in a social situation, I don't volunteer the ethnicity of my partner until it's germane to the conversation. Outside of my own cultural milieu, questions are not only OK, but often welcome; the trick sometimes lies in identifying the right way to ask. I don't claim to have never made mistakes along the way. I've offended or annoyed people without meaning to. It'll happen again. But I expect my social and romantic demographics to remain consistent. My friends are still my friends, whatever color they are; my lovers (and now my partner) are still people, not a fetish.

Not Something Tangible

SKY GILBERT

It's not something tangible; it's more like an insinuation.

Something in the air. In the way people respond—or don't.

Take the movies, for instance.

For my boyfriend and I, going to a gay film these days is much less a pleasure than an obligation. We know—however witty the dialogue is (and it usually isn't), however subtle the plot twists are (and they usually aren't), that at one point or other the romantic couple are going to be confronted with a horrible crisis. And that horrible crisis will, unfortunately, be infidelity. Of course it won't involve an indiscretion that takes place at the baths, park or toilet (real gay places where real gay men go for sex). It will be presented in straight terms—i.e., one member of the twosome will catch a stranger's eye across a crowded room. Presto: an adulterous affair. At this point my boyfriend and I are deeply disappointed and completely lose interest in the movie, for in these flicks, gay couples are invariably just like straight ones—they have the same insecurities, the same fears and they break up for the same reasons. In this unimaginative little straight world, there are no ménages, arrangements or open relationships. When homosexual men fall in love in the movies, it's for life, and not until the evil ('other man') turns the whole schlimazel into a weepy mess, is a negative note sung in their un-gay little paradise.

And it's not just the movies—it's our friends. I can count on the fingers of one hand the gay male friends with whom we can discuss the intimate details of our relationship, for we know we will have to reveal that we are open. And it is at this point that the look of disapproval flickers across their eyes. You see, these judgmental, intractable little fags just don't see our relationship as REAL. But they don't say that out loud. They are polite, tolerant (nothing is more insulting than tolerance). Their disapproval usually manifests itself as a question: "And how, umm, does an open relationship work, exactly?" And we say: "Yes, it's wonderful, and it works just great for us." "But don't you like, umm, get jealous?"

THE LOVE THAT DARE NOT SPEAK ITS NAME

they will invariable ask. And we tell them that we do—but that somehow, because we love each other, it doesn't ultimately matter. The notion
that we try desperately to get across to them is that we don't use our
sport fucking to hurt each other. We would never hurl a trick or baths
experience in the face of a lover to wound him, and we never compare
our adventures, or compete. (In fact we almost never discuss our
promiscuity. That's part of the bargain.) But no matter how many questions we get, no matter how much we explain the situation, these quiet-
ly opinionated interlopers inevitably leave the discussion more confused
and suspicious than when the talk began.

We have friends (for instance) who are fully convinced that my
lover is exploiting and hurting me. I am seventeen years older than my
boyfriend. In our ageist gay culture, such a distance is daunting, and
causes curtains to twitch. (A twitch of a curtain means a ruined reputa-
tion in this town!) My partner (let's call him "River") has friends who
will not be dissuaded from the notion that I am being abused. They don't
find older gay men attractive (I'm almost fifty). And basically, they just
can't get their tiny minds around the notion that I can, and do, get laid.
River is recently thirty, lithe, pretty, with pale skin, prominent pecs and
sparkling eyes. He still looks like a boy and gets propositioned regularly on the street and in bathhouses. I am ruggedly good-looking and built
like a football player. I'm also grim and rarely smile. The two of us make
an odd couple. We're very gay-looking. When people spot us on the
street there is absolutely no reason to imagine why we would be
together—except for, well, gay reasons. Older football players don't usually hang out with sweet looking, effeminate boys. But River's friends
won't stop nagging him. "What about Hank?" they'll say. (For now, let's
call me Hank.) How does Hank feel about you screwing around?"
"Hank likes it just fine," River will say. "In fact he screws around more
than I do." This is true. Though it's difficult, at times, to figure out who
is the bigger slut (and we try not to count the number of times we go out
cruising, separately, weekly, for sex). I am the more compulsive. And I
certainly have no trouble getting laid. (The older I get, the more I realize
how much fun I missed not being a Daddy. Though I will say that what
is required of me sexually these days involves a certain dominance
which I usually only reluctantly supply.) But no matter how much River

ESSAYS ON QUEER DESIRE AND SEXUALITY

reassures his friends that I'm more than happy with our relationship, they insist on imagining me at home, knitting and crying, setting a light in the window or just swallowing my sadness and loneliness in humble masochistic silence. Of course, in reality, I am much more likely to be swallowing the cum of a stranger (or more likely still, someone is likely to be swallowing mine).

The subtle apex of this disapproval comes in a most humiliating and ultimately irritating question, a question which both of us are destined to hear whenever we venture out into the world of gay society sans partner. We hear it if one of us visits a party without the other one, or meet a friend at the disco or bathhouse while cruising alone. I urge you never to broach this question to any member of a couple. It is so insulting, so incredibly stupid and so transparently mean, that you would be doing yourself a favor if you simply refrained. The question I'm referring to is this: "And so, where's your lover tonight?"

I happen to frequent gay discos. My lover detests them. There is a man who approaches me literally every other night when I'm out on the town. I dread the encounter. He sidles up and queries, "Where is your lover tonight?" Now in this particular case I happen to know very well that this gentleman (dare I call him that?) is a little in love with my boyfriend. But that's no surprise since this question is born from jealousy and insecurity and betrays not a trace of actual concern. Usually I am simply unable to answer. My lover and I certainly don't spend every breathing moment together, and we lead quite active lives apart from each other in every respect (not just the sexual area). So when this question is asked, I sometimes just don't know where my lover is. Often, I admit it. This, of course, will elicit an ironic and knowing accusation: "You don't know where he is? Hmm . . . is that wise?" or some such thing. The particularly barfly who so often questions me in this manner has been known to parry with an even nastier little attack: "Well it must be convenient to have a lover that you never spend any time with!"

This supposed concern about my lover's whereabouts is not concern at all. It's ill concealed disapproval. If we were GOOD lovers, then we would be together. Lovers are always together, aren't they? Except that:

a) all lovers operate differently, and

39

THE LOVE THAT DARE NOT SPEAK ITS NAME

b) lovers who insist on spending every waking moment together are usually co-dependent.

River is so annoyed by this question that he has supplied me with an all-purpose answer. When somebody cruises up to me and asks, "Where is your lover tonight?" I have been ordered to say: "He's out sucking cock in an alley."

Well, it works like a charm. I wish you could see these horrid little snoops after they've fully digested this answer. Their faces fall like a pair of old, loose underwear. They are lost in a land where the usual social niceties have been impaled on their own petards. They can't believe that I would say such a thing, and yet the sound of the phrase "out sucking cock" is for them, a strangely freeing, even empowering experience.

What if, in fact, all lovers were allowed to go out and suck cock whenever they wanted to? What would happen to romance?

And romance is the key word.

I realized this when being interrogated by yet another friend. You see I felt sorry for him; he is one of those "I can't get a lover no matter what I do" types. And he is particularly typical of that ilk—the fag who is serially promiscuous and very attractive; who, in fact, probably wouldn't be happy in a monogamous situation, but is nevertheless committed (in the part of his brain that has seen too many movies) to wishing that he had a faithful partner. At first, this fellow (another barfly) seemed impressed by our arrangement. But impressed in the way that most gay men are—his supportive comments were tainted with innuendo. I revealed the details of our relationship, quite honestly, to help him discover a way out of his loneliness. He leaned back and sighed. "It's nice to know that you've been able to do without romance." Something happened after that—I can't remember what—I may have simply staggered away drunkenly. But I never contradicted him. I may very well not have wanted to at the time. Out of concern for his feelings, I pretended I had abandoned romance.

Whenever I go out whoring—I look for this man. I want to tell him the truth. I don't care about his feelings any more. For the fact of the matter is, I am very much in love with River. Not despite the fact that he is a slut, but because of it.

There are many reasons to love River.

Let me count the ways.

First and foremost he is my soul mate.

What is a soul mate?

A person who can read your mind and speaks your thoughts without prompting.

Now, our opinions are certainly not always confluent. We often argue about films or books. But when I am fundamentally moved, fundamentally angered, River is always there. He always surprises me. I remember once when, in typically contrary fashion, he told me that he disliked music of any kind. I was surprised. (I am an opera fan, and lately I can barely rip myself away from my Verdi.) Well one night, I happened by his room (yes, we have separate bedrooms) and he was playing Kathleen Ferrier, some arrangement of a sea shanty that I happened to love. I know it seems like a small thing, but our fundamental similarities are always affirmed. And sometimes at the most unexpected moments.

Perhaps I'm not describing this accurately.

I know I'm not.

He is deeply, profoundly witty. His way of looking at the world is a mixture of morbid pessimism and ironic commentary. He hates the world and loves it deeply. He laughs at people and gossips about them constantly, but—even when he won't admit it—he loves people with a fundamental humanity. He also adores playacting, fooling, kidding and tickling. But most of all he is aware of the absurdity of human existence and enjoys poking fun at pretension. He also abhors hypocrisy (very important), but his anger is coupled with a scathing sense of humor.

I still have not told you enough.

I haven't mentioned, of course, that he is a very good person—in the Shakespearean sense—a boy whose gentle beauty matches inside and out. There is a subtle grace, a dignity to his movements (especially when he is angry) which can move me to tears and drive me irresistibly to kiss him. And kiss him I do. In elevators, in the kitchen, in bed, in the bathroom, on a walk to the subway, whenever the spirit moves me—and it moves me often. His face is so beautiful and so tender, that sometimes when I'm kissing him I feel that I am melting into it. Not that we are becoming one; because no two people could be so fundamentally different. It's just that he has the perfect face of a beautiful boy. But unlike so many other beautiful boys that I kiss, his face is not a mask that hides deception, stupidity and cruelty. It is the appropriate cover for what Oscar Wilde loved to call a "slim, gilt soul."

But now I have completely embarrassed myself, dated myself and become effusive in a typically old faggot historical/hysterical way.

I think it's important that you know that I love him because he is a slut. I could not love him if he wasn't. The fact that he courts danger, seeks adventure, steps boldly out into the night, into the dark, into the park, the alley, wherever, and offers what is sometimes mine to others — this soothes me, excites me and frightens me. It makes me feel very alive. But most of all, he understands my own obsessive forays. Not only does he not disapprove, (for let me emphasize, again, tolerance is the most insulting form of flattery) he also loves the fact that I am with other men, on my knees, on my back (whatever!) as often as humanly possible. (I won't go into pornographic detail here and perhaps this speaks to the antique and quite eccentric nature of our romance because I plan on reading this piece for him on our anniversary and I know that he would not want to hear any of my sordid details, just as I would not wish to know his.) But it is the fact that I humiliate myself, weekly, in pursuit of other men, that I satisfy what is after all just a human and quite beautiful and necessary and intimate need; that I love sex the way he does, and am addicted to receiving and giving pleasure — well, that makes all the difference.

Because if that's not what life is for, then what after all, is it all about?

But you see I have saved something for him. Not my cock and not my ass. Not my pecks and not my submissiveness. Not my cum and not my saliva. And certainly not my arousal. All that is for the world. What I have saved for him is a kind of intimacy that I couldn't possibly have with anyone else. But then again, it isn't a matter of saving it, for I don't resist giving it to someone else — no matter how good the sex, how kinky the stranger is, how much the trick meshes with some physical ideal or fantasy of fulfillment. Because what happens between River and me will always be different than what we have with anyone else. We don't have to work at it, or make it that way.

It just is.

I certainly miss him constantly and always yearn to be with him when I've been away from him for a day or two. You see, he is my Maude Gonne.

Maude Gonne was the woman that Yeats loved. I don't know if I have the history right (and I'm too lazy to look it up) but it seems to me they never consummated the affair, or if they did, it lasted only briefly. He was the famous Irish poet, of course, and she was a literary person herself, who, early on in her life, moved to France and I think got married. But Yeats always nurtured a passion for this unrequited love, and though she was literally gone (hence the irony of her name) he never had to fan the flame; it was just burned, eternally, much to his pain and her chagrin.

River is always around—I see him daily. We live together. But there is something about his promiscuity and mine which keeps him far enough way, in fact, just out of my reach, which makes me long all the more for him.

I think that Harry Hay said it best. I met him once in Provincetown, by chance, in a submarine shop. Harry flirted with me. (It is my claim to fame that Harry Hay, the founder of the Mattachine Society and modern gay liberation, flirted with ME! I will never tire of telling this story again and again, always in different ways . . .). The eminent gay activist was in his eighties, accompanied by his lover, John. He turned to me and with a glint in his eye said, "I could leave John—at any moment—if someone better came along." (And his smile was as shy and alluring as a man of his age and experience could muster.) "We are not married, we are not committed in that traditional way, that's just the kind of relationship we have."

Of course, I didn't run off with Harry Hay. I don't think he would have actually wanted me to. But I also know he meant what he said. He meant it completely, and he meant it not at all. Harry Hay has the kind of relationship with his lover where he is deeply close to him all the time, and also deeply far away.

And that is what makes love work.

At least, that's what I think.

Have I thoroughly confused you now?

The Etiology and Lost Art of "The Quickie"

FELICE PICANO

There was a time, and it doesn't seem so long ago to some of us, when sex wasn't all that serious: We had drugs like penicillin and all kinds of new preventative antibiotics to take care of STDs, and even consensual-contact problems such as crabs, scabies, herpes and warts were—if not always easy to get rid of—problems one could cope with. Women had the pill to avoid pregnancy. As a result, and probably for the first time in human history, sex had few physical ramifications—and if one was only moderately observant—no life-long consequences. Sex wasn't dangerous or, seldom of itself, fatal. Sex was a game, a toy, a charm, a fun kind of thing to do. As a result—sex involved, (for some of us), mystery, impulse, experimentation, abandon, and often satisfaction to the point of exhaustion.

That was before AIDS, of course.

Three friends and I formed a birthday club in 1976. We met for the next five years, several times a year, treating each other to the best and often the most expensive restaurants in Manhattan and its environs (one foray to Westchester, one to Brooklyn Heights). We ate wonderfully and not surprisingly, during each birthday dinner, we told stories about the past few months. Two male birthdays were close together in February, often celebrated concurrently, one female birthday in May, another in November.

I can't recall which of us first brought up the idea of talking about our "quickies," our most spontaneous and usually our fastest sexual encounters. But the subject did come up, and first Jane then I told of our own recent quickies. Susan claimed to have less sex than the rest of us, and she certainly was more discreet about it. But what she may have lacked in flash she compensated for in shock value: she would end up sleeping with the most unlikely characters: a boss, a client, once an executive she was interviewing for. Little stood in her way: she went after and got the long time boyfriend of her best friend. Compared to her, we all looked like pikers.

By the following conjointly celebrated birthday I had my quickie story all ready and so did the others, except, as usual, Susan. In fact, we all began to look forward to this lurid new addition to our little galas. There's something about discussing in carefully chosen detail one's sex act within the all-encompassing atmosphere of cultivation and sophistication that adds piquancy, not only to the story itself, but also to the Grand Mariner Hazelnut Floating Island one is demolishing, and to the B&B one is sipping. The first time I realized this was a decade earlier. My South Indian gay doctor from Brazil with extravagant social pretensions dragged me on a double date with a celebrated society woman and her fashion model daughter. I was still flirting with bisexuality at the time, and for the next few months I indifferently dated the lovely, verve-deficient mannequin. Our few attempts at love-making foundered completely on her wet-noodle response: she really did just lay there. Naturally I presumed that when I stopped phoning, it was with the understanding that our electricity level was below the capacity of any scale to measure. I was astonished when her mother phoned and invited me to lunch at one of the city's few Four Star restaurants, Caravelle. There, the middle-aged, beautiful, quite vital woman asked me why I wasn't seeing her daughter. I told her I was gay. She relaxed instantly and we became good buddies. After choosing desserts, I mentioned that one of them resembled the penis of my last male partner and put my hands up before myself to show her how big he was. To which she reacted with mock-horror. Pushing my hands down, she lifted one hand, palm down, above the expensive linen tablecloth to demonstrate the same length, saying, "Always do it this way. People will think you're discussing a vase." Recalling our lewd conversation, amid socialites and business moguls, tickled me for years to come.

It was just days before the third-year February meeting of the Birthday Club that I encountered a young man in Grand Central Station. He was slender, blond, well dressed and evidently gay. He looked pointedly at my crotch. I'd come from a record store nearby and was headed downstairs to the cross-town shuttle, leading to my own subway downtown. He came up close and made a better suggestion: why not go up

THE LOVE THAT DARE NOT SPEAK ITS NAME

into the building he worked in, at that time the newly constructed Met Life insurance building that had been appended to the northern end of the terminal, rising some sixty stories behind and above it. I agreed. In the elevator-ride up, filled with office workers returning from lunch, he looked more and more attractive. While small, he certainly fit that gray suit well. I was horny with anticipation when we reached a floor and got out. He moved far from me, gesturing with a hand behind that I ought to keep my distance. Then he waited until the others had filtered into their offices before gesturing me forward in the long corridor through a doorway. The stairway occupied an exposed side of the building, giant louvers with sunlight filtering in at angles. I could look down some fifteen stories and up an equal number of stairways. It was visually and spatially magnificent. Even better: "No one ever uses this," he assured me, then pulled me down halfway between the landing, where he sat down and opened my pants.

As with most quickies, I had only a few seconds to decide the following: 1) Am I that horny? 2) Is this guy that hot? and 3) What are the chances we get caught?

This time, however, I found that I had two more additional decisions to make, based on two entirely new criteria: 1) Will this make a good quickie story next week at the Birthday dinner? and 2) Is this not one of the most stylish Architectural Digest sites to get a blow job?

Obviously the extra time needed meant that he already had my zipper down and my dick in his mouth by the time I could make up my mind. Thus, I had my quickie, and the following week it was very well received at dinner.

By then of course, all of the Birthday Club members, even the usually non-contributing Susan, had become connoisseurs of the quickie. We knew exactly what constituted a good one: it had to be spontaneous; the partner had to be a stranger (but this wasn't inflexible); there should be an element of risk or danger of discovery to it (although that wasn't the *reason* to do it); and the nuttier, the more dramatic, or the more improbable the setting, the better. It was of course assumed that you were horny and attracted to the guy, and that the two of you were in some way egging each other on. As far as quickies went, those were the criteria.

ESSAYS ON QUEER DESIRE AND SEXUALITY

I'd be lying if I said I'd never had quickies before the Birthday Club began to meet. In the 1960s and early 1970s, whenever I had gay sex it was *de facto*, a quickie. My first adult blow job at age 18 happened in the basement men's room of the Walt Whitman Hall (English Department) at Queens College, City University of New York where I matriculated. I was reading on the can when a scrawled piece of toilet paper suddenly slid into view on the tiles below me, followed by the much-bitten stub of a #3 pencil. I read, "Blow job?" and wondered whether I was to give or receive, then looked at the shoes of the person in the next booth and for some reason mollified, wrote back, "OK." He then scribbled back, "Come!"

I pulled up my denims, went into his booth and saw a nice enough looking red-haired student with a very crimson-tipped stiff dick. The minute I got in, he locked the door, all but ripped open my pants and sucked me off like a starving man. When I came, I floated to the ceiling. I'm sorry to say I did not return the favor when he asked, but instead wafted up and out of the building and thus into the rest of my life.

Over the following year and a half of college, I frequented this bathroom occasionally and scored a few more blow jobs but never again from him, nor as good, before discovering the Paul Klapper Library across the quad had better cocksuckers—a definitively hetero pal said he got off there regularly—while the new science building proved to be even better. While I certainly put myself directly into the path of pleasure, I was always astounded when the act somehow actually happened. One time, the brainiest guy in my The Calculus of Physics class was blowing me when there was a tap on our toilet booth door. I began to panic, but not him; instead, he let in the *second* brainiest guy in the class who immediately dropped to the tiles to blow the first one while I was brought off. When I got up to leave, still amazed by the fact that three of us had fit into the booth student number two had gotten up and was now busily settling his attractive rear end onto student number one's penis, with various rotational motions and small sighs. Doubtless, attempting to verify for himself a variety of Euclidiean and Newtonian laws.

When I was a social worker in the Vista Program, I had a twenty-minute by local, or a shorter and far more crowded subway ride directly up to the East Side Welfare and Childcare Center where I had my office-base. Even on the local I seldom got a seat and usually settled for finding a pole to wrap myself around so I could read and ignore what was happening around me in the crush. Often I was still half asleep. Imagine my surprise when, one morning, I felt an unusual crush on the local and found myself at the end of a car tightly wedged between two presentable, tall, identical male twins with light brown hair, both of whom—when I finally got enough distance to actually check—wore what looked like ski-lift wear. Actually, I felt them before I saw them. Felt hands on my front and on my back, felt a rubbing across my corduroy trouser front, and a hand slipping in between my buns. In seconds, I was as if surrounded, and quickly and rather expertly—they must have done a few every morning to arrive at such proficiency—I was manually manipulated and massaged through the material to orgasm, by one or the other, or both, I couldn't tell. All the while, they seemed to concentrate on subway ads high above my head, while less than a foot away, people sat and read newspapers or novels, while only a *few inches* away, other people stood (protecting the two) trying to shift their weight or to getter a better hold on the horizontal bars above, totally oblivious to our three-way sex.

Just as I felt the wetness spreading across my thigh, the doors opened and the twins were gone in a rushing swirl of crowd. I was brought off one more time by these trouser-marauders, almost equally unaware what was happening, and I caught them doing the same to other guys twice more. The last time, I got off the train when they did and followed them onto another car, where I offered myself to them and they "had" me again, in their usual, fast, baffling, absolutely expert way. But by then I knew they preferred getting guys who weren't onto them. That was part of their thrill.

During most of my misguided twenties I searched for love and romance. What a ghastly decade *that* turned out to be. Luckily, towards the end of that delusion, I managed to talk myself (and a few others) into believing I was a writer, thus replacing a common delusion with a somewhat less common one. With the result that like the ballerina heroine of my favorite Edward Gorey saga-in-miniature, *The Gilded Bat*, I began to live for art, and once again, take sex whenever and wherever it showed

ESSAYS ON QUEER DESIRE AND SEXUALITY

itself.

The first time this occurred was uptown during lunchtime. I'd gone to work as part-time Christmas help for Doubleday Bookstores (how temporary can you get?) and I'd been assigned to the Grand Central Station outlet. I first worked in the slow, smaller shop on the west side of the terminal, which really only got a little busy at rush hours, including lunchtime. Then, I suppose because I demonstrated a smidgen of competence, I was moved to the slightly larger but far busier, East Side shop, astoundingly busy during lunchtime and rush hour. Directly below that shop was the stock room, and next to it, the changing room for employees at the "world-famous" Oyster Bar. This consisted of a few lockers on opposing walls with a central narrow bench. It was shown to me when I was given a general tour of the place by the manager.

Later on, when I became more familiar with the area as I began restocking books for the shop, I noticed yet another doorway, and a man dressed as though he were a railroad engineer coming out of it from what seemed to me to be a steep stairway even further down than these, three floors below street level. The stockroom manager introduced me to the engineer who took me through the mysterious door on a tour of the large open spaces beneath the terminal, including railroad tracks and a tunneled pedestrian pathway with emergency lights a hundred feet below the already sunken commuter and Amtrak tracks. It was hollowed out during the early years of World War II, he told me, and led from 42nd Street south to the basement level of the Empire State building, then north up Park Avenue before it bent left to Rockefeller Center and St. Patrick's Cathedral. I never discovered if this was true or not, but he said it was built in case of Nazi jet airplane development and the air bombing of New York. It would be an escape route from major population centers to unhit areas, and safe haven from falling bombs, as the London and Berlin subway platforms had proven to be.

During one lunchtime walk outside the huge terminal, I met a very hunky construction worker who read my interest in him. We walked for ten minutes, then he asked for sex and where we could go. I didn't know of the stairways of Met Life yet. All I could think of was the changing room for the Oyster Bar. There I blew him. He left first, and as I was leaving, an employee saw me and demanded to know what I was doing

49

THE LOVE THAT DARE NOT SPEAK ITS NAME

there. He'd not seen the construction worker leave, I guess, and I suppose he thought I was trying to break into the lockers. I told him I worked in the bookstore and was resting. He didn't believe me. A month later as I was stepping out of the stockroom with an armload of books, I encountered him again. I guess because he wasn't as fearful and angry, he looked more appealing, and had a Greek-American accent. He again asked what I was doing though he could see for himself I worked for the bookstore. He half-jokingly voiced his earlier suspicion. I knew I was being transferred to another bookstore location in a few weeks so I blurted out I wasn't a thief, but that I'd brought a guy down from the street to suck his cock. The cook looked startled and in his confusion I got away.

A few days later he came into the book shop, late in the afternoon and waited until we were alone. He asked me to come by his station behind the clam bar at a certain time the next day and he'd treat me to as many oysters as I wanted for free. When I asked why, he touched his crotch and said he knew I would return the favor. I did go, and got several dozen oysters, cooked a variety of ways, including the famous—but only so-so—Oysters Rockefeller. He must have eaten a few too. Because later, down in the changing room, he came pretty quickly.

This kind of quickie activity was limited to at-work. At home, my personal life was *l'amour, l'amour*, with the concomitant tragic-comic results going on for years.

What I hadn't for an instant suspected was that around age twenty-nine or so I'd begun approaching whatever apogee of physical attractiveness I would ever possess. I'd put some weight onto my skin and bones and my face no longer resembled a "wounded, insomniac Koala Bear," as one friend described me, or a "badly shattered Giotto St. John mural," as another had. It was the mid-1970s, the sexual revolution, and suddenly sex was anywhere, everywhere I looked, and didn't look. I was living in the West Village, and so at times all I had to do was walk to my front door to get sex. I used to joke that I walked twenty feet from my ground floor apartment door on Jane Street to get my m. a. i. l. and also came back with m. a. l. e.—in this case sitting on the steps awaiting someone else. A guy who rang my bell awakening me one Saturday morning to tell me smoke was coming out of the basement remained for

50

ESSAYS ON QUEER DESIRE AND SEXUALITY

impromptu sex. I was still in my underwear, when the Fire Department arrived. A telephone repairman working in the back yard, ended up indoors for sex.

Late at night, I'd come home from a movie, dinner with others, a party, and sit on my brownstone stoop. People would pass, coming from the subway headed home or to one of the large newer apartment buildings, and stop for a chat and end up coming in for more. Cars would stop, the drivers would get out, and if I liked them, they'd look for nearby parking. All I did was sit there. In this manner, and among many others, I bagged: 1) a well known Hollywood movie star, 2) two Broadway theater actors of note, 3) three well-known visual artists, 4) three composers (two classical, one theatrical), and 5) a male nurse on his night off, who was caring for Tennessee Williams, a few blocks away.

Strolling the 'Village late at night on pleasant evenings I'd meet people. Now that area is trafficked 24 hours a day. Then it was empty, New York City close to bankruptcy, the population smaller than any time since the 1930s, so there was less risk of discovery, and because of the freewheeling attitudes of the era, fewer people felt they should judge you for having public sex—what if they wanted to do the same? One particularly attractive man I'd been checking out for months became available for ten minutes at two-thirty a.m. on West Fourth Street between 11th and Perry streets. The problem was his lover, awaiting him on the third floor. So I did him on the stairway, in a tree-dimmed area, but visible to anyone, really. It was pretty daring. But I didn't care. Neither did he.

Another time walking home from the Eagle's Nest bar in the far west 20s, I encountered a well-built man in his forties, dressed as though he was out sex hunting and acting like he hadn't gotten any yet. We'd both crossed 14th Street to Hudson Street, and as I passed him, he was putting out killer-pheromones that screamed, "Fuck me!" I walked past, turned, saw him walk between two parked trucks in a loading dock, joined him and did what he wished, twelve feet from street traffic. Later, when a friend was arrested in an Act-Up demonstration and I went to bail him out, this same hot guy I'd so memorably porked was the presiding judge. I wondered if he'd remember me. He did and let my friend go without bail, in my "recognizance." I wrote the scene in *Like*

51

THE LOVE THAT DARE NOT SPEAK ITS NAME

People in History.

I can hear you asking, OK, then which time was it *not* a complete stranger? For years, the wooden decks of ocean liner piers otherwise fallen down or been demolished continued to totter along the Hudson River, not far from where I lived most of my time in the West Village. After work, or afternoons, I'd go out to a pier to read, sun, cool down, or people-watch. One afternoon a cute young guy picked me up. We went back to my place where he all but raped me in his passion. I saw him several times more, and only on the last occasion did he show me the text he'd been studying: High School Geometry Regent Exams. He was that young. He looked much older, told me he'd had gay sex since he was eight, and a lover in the Bronx since he was twelve. A period of travel for me meant I lost track of him a few years. One night, my barber, Julio Velez had tickets to a recital by Spanish soprano Monserrat Caballe at Lincoln Center and invited me. We were very excited and got there early. Center row seats, six rows from the stage. We were both psyched. Five minutes before the performance, I went to the men's room. Coming out I saw my formerly underaged trick, Pete. He looked sexy in usher uniform and seeing me, he popped a boner. Only one thing to do, he dragged me into a sort of janitor's closet set in back of the orchestra seats. We kissed, necked, blew each other. Great sex. But then, we couldn't get out! We were locked in! He was about to start banging for help, when the door swung open. Sweating, flushed, relieved, I rushed down to the seat, where Julio was fuming: how dare I be late! During the first round of applause, after her Vivaldi arias, I told him what happened, and Julio, a man of the world, forgave me instantly.

And the all-time wildest quickie I ever had? New Year's Eve. Manhattan. I was unattached and had been to several tedious parties and ended up in The Eagle's Nest, where one really interesting guy would pass by, touch me lightly, say two words, then move on. This went on for an hour and it was getting on 3:30 a.m. Ten minutes later, I tried to get his attention to tell him I was leaving. No dice. So I left. Outside, it was strangely warmer. It began to snow. No cabs waiting outside, so I'd walk. I did, checking out guys making it in doorways all along 22nd Street. I'd reached 10th Avenue when I heard noise behind me: the guy I'd been cruising, calling me. I moved on, waited, moved on

52

ESSAYS ON QUEER DESIRE AND SEXUALITY

more, and waited.

By the time he reached me, snow was falling heavily. Cars came at the rate of about one-per-ten minutes. He said something, and frustrated, I said he should make up his mind whether he wanted me or not. He said he did, but couldn't go home with me. Annoyed, I unzipped and took it out right there in the middle of the avenue.

"You want it? Do it now. Here!"

He knelt down in the middle of the street and did. The two cars that passed us while I stood in the heavy snow-pour swerved extravagantly not to hit us, blinking their headlights extravagantly, pressing their horns loudly, the occupants drunkenly shouting out of half cracked-open windows, "Happy New Year."

That was a quickie! Too bad my Birthday Club had suspended its meetings.

(very) Trying Monogamy

ROYSTON TESTER

In the early hours of a Sunday morning—after twelve hours and twice that number of guys—I was heading home along the Queen Elizabeth Way rerunning the wildest moments of a night spent in steam room fivesomes, cubicles and abandoned fucks in the sling. Poppers, lube, dope. You'd think I'd had enough. But hitting the lakeshore highway out of Toronto, I felt so aroused that my grip on the wheel was itching to turn back for another shift at St. Marc's Spa. I was in my late twenties, new to Canada, a working-class English boy who'd "escaped" to North America; high on tricking and an off-on boyfriend called Bill. Everything beyond the world of showers, semi-erect men in towels prowling dimly lit corridors, seemed devastatingly ordinary. Why would I want an empty bed when, just minutes back, there were hot bodies pleading for cock? I grabbed at my bag and yanked the zipper.

That longing to come and come.

In the overtaking lane, window down, I let the November chill roar through the car; I slapped at my dick and felt like a god. If going homeward it was—some inner voice telling me, "Rest. Get some sleep, man"—then I'd turn this goddamn road into some action, beforehand.

It didn't take long.

Up ahead was an old model truck, just high enough above my Honda for the driver to see right into my lap.

He was around my age—curly-headed, pimply. I accelerated slightly, until the car was alongside, then touched the brake and let him take a good look at the passer-by, whose stiffy basked in the lights from the dash.

Not for a moment did I think, "What if he's straight, a queer-basher or some blackbelt? Are you nuts?" I wanted to see what the guy would do. I shook my dick back and forth. And after a minute or so of cruising, drove the car several vehicles ahead, and waited.

Farmboy—let's call him that—didn't waste much time.

At the airport turn-off he indicated right; and as he passed me on the

ESSAYS ON QUEER DESIRE AND SEXUALITY

inside, took in his cock-teaser.

Expressionless, this bloke neither wanted me to pursue; nor stay where I was.

On he went.

And I followed.

In a recent *Gay.comUK* interview, Jason Jones interviewed David—a 38-year-old businessman who's had sex with more men than he can count. Monogamy bores him. "Isn't it about the person you're with and not the body?" asks Jones. "That's a bit naïve," replies our man on the town. Does David think monogamy is possible at all, then? "I don't think it's a viable option for interesting people." It's about sophistication and being "evolved," according to him. "What about love?" says the interviewer. "Love is just a word that's bandied about to deny our true nature . . . . The last relationship I had a couple of years back was open, but it didn't work because love breeds sexual jealousy and eventually that destroys everything. Love destroys everything."

For many gay men, David's kind of thinking is the reason they turn to monogamy. In him they see the compulsive cycle of bar-hopping, one-night stands, phone games, body-fascism, circuit parties and breathtaking highs and lows that arguably strain our capacity for faithful, long-standing commitment. How much more preferable to find trust and stability in a monogamous relationship, even if the sex does get a tad perfunctory after a year or so. Who wants to be chasing cock day-in day-out? Do we have the time and energy? Can't we contain sexual jealousy? Use it as dirty talk for our own in-house romps with a lifemate?

What about intimacy, the shared life, kids even, a caring, responsive partner who will always be there? Isn't this "sophisticated" and "evolved" too? Isn't it also the "true nature" of a queer man? We recognize love in it. Something that means more than "fuck." These are also the romanticized views of queer neo-conservatives, Sex Panic adherents and marriage-touting radicals. Arguments that draw us all to some sort of conclusion: a stance.

Trouble is, monogamy doesn't work.

At best it's a decent fantasy. No-one can live up to its demands, or worse, people—gay and straight—without much if any reflection, accept

55

THE LOVE THAT DARE NOT SPEAK ITS NAME

it as the right way to build a relationship, even if its dictates remove happiness and pleasure from their union. It's seen as the foundation of family values, and any questioning of it invites censure or wariness. Mainstream society deplores sharing, even though 85% of human cultures—before the Judeo-Christian homogenization—were polygynous. Males of all species—and this is why I focus on queer *males* rather than lesbians—are especially poor at monogamy. Even in 1978 "in the face of AIDS," according to New York queer-activist Jim Eigo "only 14% of gay American men were in monogamous relationships."

The word itself is inappropriate to gay male culture—and for this essay.

A monogamist—unlike, say, a bigamist, digamist or polygamist—is, according to my Oxford dictionary, "One who disallows second marriage . . . refraining or disbarred from marriage after the death of the first spouse." In fact it's the *zoological* definition that gets closer to how most use the term: "the habit of living in pairs"—which situates us with ape and ostrich, apparently. "Non-monogamy" it doesn't list at all. But "promiscuous" is there: "casual, careless, irregular," "term of contempt or depreciation," "confusion," "sexual union, as among some of the races of *low civilization*." (My italics.) Also, "without order, method or respect for kind."

Such a happening word.

But the best of its definitions and the one I'd like to use here is: *"rarely of a single thing."* Promiscuity is about pluralities, diversity and how we choose to manage them. As psychologist Adam Phillips puts it in *Monogamy*, " . . . we do not know whether we want monogamy, but we do know that we fear excess: an excess of solitude and an excess of company. We are not, of course, naturally monogamous. We are the animals for whom something is too much." In fact, in our love relationships we live in this tension between the "rarely of a single thing" condition (call it the will to promiscuity) and "monogamy" (the desire for pairdom).

But let's first rid ourselves of the trappings of zoology and the overtones of heterosexual marriage inherent in the word "monogamy." As it stands, it's rather like one of the "literary" texts Alan Sinfield describes in his *Cultural Politics - Queer Reading* because it contests "aspects of our

ESSAYS ON QUEER DESIRE AND SEXUALITY

ideological formation." There's an "awkward, unresolved" fault line running right through "monogamy." We need to rework its story—and employ another signifier. After all, without a distinct and germane language about our queerness, we're invisible, so I'm going to call our topic "magnolia" instead of "monogamy." It was that or "moniscuity"—but moniscuity approximates the original word with its connotations of the "monolithic" and "mono" (as in "That bastard's given me . . . ") and "monotony" (the businessman David's hang-up). And I didn't go for "promogamy," which has "progrom" lurking in its genes and sounds like another disease.

Magnolia still represents a concern for pairing; but in a newer way, along the lines of "modified," "responsible" or "postmodern" monogamy espoused by commentators like Signorile in *Life Outside* and any number of gay-positive psychotherapists and social workers; acknowledging the role of third parties in a couple's relationship.

Let's stay with promiscuity as the word of opposition. Unlike magnolia it declares a fundamental interest in plurality for its own sake (rather than as a way of sustaining a *couple*): multiple partners, the polyamorous life (distributed commitment, "couple-three" as poly theorist Bernadette Bosky puts it, any number of genders, orientations). Nothing to do with "contempt" or the "irregular." Simply a way of forming intimate or casual relationships where the notion of "pair" in a life-long commitment is not entertained.

So . . . magnolia or promiscuity?

In the darkness of a service road he pulled over into a factory driveway and stopped.

Now what?

Like a schoolboy on bennies, I rubbed the head of my cock and realized that if I wanted to hook-up I was going to have to act. Stuffing the saliva-wet dick inside my pants, I opened the door to get out. But as the interior light went on, farmboy was already at the passenger side and climbing in. "Hi," he said, settling himself into the seat like an old friend. He was making a point of not looking at my crotch. "I was at my girlfriend's," I said, just in case he turned ugly. "Yeah, me too."

We both looked ahead at the warehouse and some mind-numbing amber

57

THE LOVE THAT DARE NOT SPEAK ITS NAME

lights above it. I squirmed in the seat and opened my legs wider.

"You want me to put my mouth around it?" he said.

Without a word, I undid the goods and let him taste. I stroked his tangled hair that smelled of french fries, and reached under the skinny body for his hard-on. Not missing a beat, with his spare hand he eased down the baggy pants and offered me a slab of cut meat: fattest I'd seen all night.

Neither of us took much time to come.

We wiped it on our own legs and zippered up.

Half smiles.

"Better be going," he muttered, climbing out of the car, not looking back. I wanted to speak but couldn't think of anything.

From the driveway I watched him start the four-by-four, touch the brakes a few times — kind of winky farewell — and pull away.

"That was unbelievable!" I muttered, flabbergasted at my own daring, and the farmboy's readiness.

This guy had fuelled a leviathan. In 1982, I felt invincible. Uncool to a tee. And there seemed to be no stopping. Not a thought of my boyfriend Bill or what he might be doing that night. I was drunk on sex and conquering.

No one was ever enough.

Choosing between magnolia and promiscuity is not easy. (Some would argue not necessary, either.) Just look at the factors influencing a choice: gender-role conditioning, age, peer-group, socio-economic level, family-of-origin, moral training, current response to queer subculture; not to mention your particular vulnerabilities, emotional needs and sexual and relationship history. To boot, there's more than one postructural theory to help you into a stupefying confusion and any kind of assured behaviour.

Take the influential French philosopher Jacques Derrida, for instance. If the magnolia/promiscuity issue were a text, as a good deconstructionist he would point to the fact that between two apparent binary opposites—in this case magnolia and promiscuity—there is *complicity.* Either/or deconstructs into both/and. In other words, the two unreliable terms are deeply implicated in one another; you have your cake and eat it.

To make matters better, worse (or both), the equally prominent

ESSAYS ON QUEER DESIRE AND SEXUALITY

French psychoanalyst Jacques Lacan would have us consider that once we leave the pre-Oedipal, non-verbal state of babyhood, we are left with "*a lack.*" This in turn creates *desire* or a deeply felt longing that is never fulfilled. In life we satisfy that lack with "symbolic substitutes."

Is magnolia one of these substitutes? Filling in for where mother left off? Is promiscuity? An insatiable hungering for one joyful, exciting possibility after another? A nostalgic anchorage—umbilical cord, milk-spattered teat—where we feel snug and fulfilled? Is that why both magnolia and promiscuity never entirely feel like *the answer*?

As theoretical constructions—and practice—all they offer is a leaky repository for what we felt was lost in childhood (safety, predictability, home and thrill of recognition).

In the winter of 1996, the North African sun had done little to appease the black dogs of my life gone very awry. After two months of careless, dangerous fucking, hash and anguished writing, in March I'd left my rented flat in the medina of Atlantic port-city Essaouira, south of Casablanca, and headed back to Barcelona where I once lived. Here, amongst friends, I recuperated not only from an intestinal bug acquired in Morocco, but from what had precipitated the entire expedition.

The previous December in Canada, after a twelve-year "monogamy" with Lee, we had ended our relationship in a tearful, wrenching decision that has disrupted our lives irrevocably. In fact, the final two or three years of our time together were more of a paralysis: sexual boredom, ill-concealed trysts, affairs and phone-sex with anonyms—a failure of any meaningful negotiation. We had loved each other and couldn't bear seeing what was happening.

Tragically, our accumulated frustrations—the little cruelties and neglect—created straws that eventually broke our backs. Lee even wrote a scholarly paper on the dial-a-dick period: "Is it the real thing?" he asked the assembled delegates. At the time I thought it real enough. In retrospect it was our cry for help. But we never really examined a way forward. Like the blizzards and frigidity outside our prairie lodgings that winter, Lee and I drifted into a ghastly living death. Whiteout. Paradoxically, we were both teaching "communications" to college students.

A week later—and on sabbatical—I was in Birmingham, England for Christmas with my mother, a widow. After a few days of ill-concealed despair

59

and transatlantic calls from friends, I spilled the beans about our break up. Marjorie's response: "You're better off alone, son. I never liked him." At the time, whatever she'd said would likely have seemed wrong. She was a thwarted woman: product of the Depression, Second World War, abusive stepfamily and an alcoholic father and husband. What was wounding was her contention — unbeknownst to me in all the years of her visiting us in Canada — that homosexuality was "wrong and unnatural."

Stung by the bigotry — and her brutalizing refusal to offer any consolation — I left the Midlands house and a memory of Xmas lunch spent in silence, overseen by a neglected frozen sock on the washing-line outside. She had wanted "nothing controversial" in her house. This too was a relationship that had run its course. Flush with rage and a sadness so deep it felt almost companionable, I headed for Morocco. I'll write all this out, I told myself.

And off Controversy went.

In a Barcelona sauna in March, recovered from the stomach bug, I missed the lewdness of Essaouira: the easy and frequent pick-ups; the sheer horniness of all the men around. I was 41-years-old. I knew I was drifting, just as Lee and I had stumbled through the last few years of our relationship. All I had to show was a first collection of short stories — ominously entitled Hands Over The Body — and the distinct sense that I'd wasted twelve years of my life with one man.

And here in a bathhouse, wasting even more.

With these kinds of theoretical underpinnings, magnolia/promiscuity are paths not easily walked unless we consider them provisional; as evolutionary stages along a continuum. We're preconditioned to experience both. When — or whether — we do so, depends on how free and uncompromised we are. Or think we are. As Kevin Lano determines in Breaking the Barriers to Desire, "Capitalism and Western religions have emphasized monogamy as a means of controlling and confining sexuality within a strictly reproductive mode and, formally, as a means of establishing clear (property-owning) male lines of descent." Most would agree that human beings are capable of loving and desiring more than one person, however. As the aphoristic Adam Phillips says, "It may be reassuring, but it is in fact very demanding (and often cruel) to assume that only one person can fulfil our needs." Moreover, after ten years of third-party-

ESSAYS ON QUEER DESIRE AND SEXUALITY

open magnolia, a period of unfettered promiscuity—or solitude—might seem very appealing. After a spate of triangulated lovers, a single partner might be just the ticket.

To quote Phillips again, "There is comfort in danger. This is the truth that the monogamist dreads, and the unfaithful rarely let themselves notice." In the spirit of Derrida and Lacan then, magnolia and promiscuity are really just inextricably wedded symbols of what we long for—and will never find. We only have to look at the lengths to which a magnoliaceous couple will go to avert all-out promiscuity. Take Joe for instance, who wrote his story on the internet: "Our monogamy has to do with our spiritual partnership and commitment, but we do invite guests to our bedroom from time to time and we are willing to participate in 'hug parties.'"

Joe's not so untypical. Nor was businessman David who hit upon sexual jealousy as the main obstacle to love. If you're into magnolia, you've tackled this issue head on. Or know you should whenever that culturally specific nagging comes a-calling, encapsulated even in the title of social scientist Maria Pallotta-Chiarolli's essay, 'Choosing Not To Choose: Beyond Monogamy, Beyond Duality.'

In queer communities there is no shortage of advice on how to shape magnolia into something that appeals to a given couple: cautious, highly regulated trials in extracurricular sex; out-of-town fooling around is OK; Wednesday nights off; threesomes. Maybe Kevin Lano's comment ringing in our ears, from 'The History of Non-Monogamous Lifestyles,' that "presently in some Asian cultures, 'love' has been regarded as akin to insanity." So why not a mad-shag every once in a while? Every therapist will stress the importance of honesty in these negotiated journeys into the Other; and of not overdoing any passion for rules. (Some relationships do end, after all, and no amount of hard work will resuscitate them.) A counsellor will also emphasize that these excursions are designed to strengthen the couple's relationship—and are meant to be fun.

Unfucked, I was preparing to get dressed when a well-built guy in his twenties pushed open my cubicle door and asked to come in. He looked like a Spaniard from the south: long eyelashes, glittery eyes—a line of coke may have helped.

THE LOVE THAT DARE NOT SPEAK ITS NAME

Without much prompting—and feeling oh-so-"bottom"—I lay back on the bed and we began a hungry passion. Deftly he lubed my ass as we rolled about. Pressing the head of his dick against my hole, he waited . . . kissing urgently, nibbling my ear, moaning.

Quite effortlessly, as he pressed his lips harder against mine, he slipped his tongue into my mouth and simultaneously his slender arrowdick into my ass.

I've never forgotten it.

His Andalucian bull's balls thwacking at my crack.

More importantly, when we'd finished—for nearly an hour I'd been stroking the muscle-fed 'serpent around a palm tree' tattoo that ran from his thigh to ankle—I asked his name.

"Jésus," he replied.

My eyes welled at the sheer incongruity of it, and the shattering relief. He liked older men, he said, cuddling me tight. Jésus was my one and only fuck that afternoon in the Bruch baths.

And it was everything.

Later, even when I saw Jésus picking up his next middle-aged fuckbunny I thought that maybe the gods were with me. Or at least a son. How about getting on that plane to Toronto, I told myself in the euphoric aftermath. Forgive and forget Lee and Marjorie. You've done the self-loathing-abandoned bit in a kasbah. Just look how brilliant WELL-BEING feels. The incredibly nurturing Barcelona family, my wise Moroccan pals, Jésus, the Canadian friends back home whose messages made their way to Calle San Juan. They'd all been riding with that slithery tattoo. I was up for air.

But no amount of advice will prepare anyone for David the businessman's preoccupation: *sexual jealousy.* How comfortable are you imagining—or witnessing—your beloved man kissing, sucking off, penetrating or receiving another bloke? You may be jealous of many things to do with your domestic partner (his looks, income, career, background and social skills) but would you get him to change them or give them up, even if he could? No? Then why interfere in his sexual practice?

When you change the rules in a magnoliaceous relationship, the impact is profound and often irreversible. Moreover, if the relationship is already collapsing, sex outside will not help. A third person entails the risk of your partner falling in love; or finding a "better" person to com-

62

ESSAYS ON QUEER DESIRE AND SEXUALITY

mit to. In living the authentic magnolia, you have to be fully prepared for what you'll see—and its implications.

As Jack Morin, a San Francisco psychotherapist reminds his couple-clients: for the (open) magnolia relationship to work, the parties must have "a higher than average tolerance for change, confusion, anxiety, jealousy and other extremely uncomfortable feelings." You need good-will, no lingering hurts or polarized views about issues of magnolia/promiscuity. More than anything the relationship is primary.

It's Dr. Asher who especially warns that if you live as a couple, yet include other sexual partners, there are two provisos: if you're seeking validation of your sex appeal outside the relationship, maybe you need to reconsider your motivation. If living an open relationship is about confirming self-worth rather than satisfying libido—if your sexual wandering has nothing to do with maintaining the marriage and everything to do with filling an unexplained void, then "seek help."

Sometimes, Dr. Asher advises that people in official, magnolia relationships use outside sexual activity to express dissatisfaction with something happening—or not happening—in the relationship. "Poor communication is the problem; not the need for outside sex per se."

In our own lives, whether we choose magnolia/promiscuity or decline to make any decision at all, the final word most usefully goes to the notion of creative destabilization in any choice of relationship.

At Easter 1998, I declined to attend my mother's funeral in England. The most difficult decision of my life seeing as I was her one child, albeit adopted; and there were no relatives. Ungrateful offspring, I know—"crueller than a serpent's tooth;" and today, I would behave differently. But her death—like the ending of my relationship with Lee—was caught up with such resentful, angry undercurrents that I was unable to pretend any love or respect. My first news of trouble, days before she succumbed, was her neighbour's message on the answering machine, "Hello, Royston. This is Sylvia. Your mother's in intensive care at Selly Oak and I don't think she'll be coming out. I thought you should know. Cheerio, then."

At the time, I was living in a north Toronto condominium and a deceitful monogamy with a new man, George. Far too spontaneously, we'd moved in together—and after only three months, we'd agreed on separation. I'd found a

63

THE LOVE THAT DARE NOT SPEAK ITS NAME

downtown apartment for the following month.

On the day of Marjorie's cremation over in England, I left George to his accounting and drove to the Beaches area of Toronto. Strolling the boardwalk I reflected on her life; tried to think positively; forgave the worst.

And tossed a stone into the water.

Prior to that walk, however, fired up like a spring thaw I'd visited St. Marc's Spa. In the middle of the afternoon, I'd approached the only person there: a black guy, 30's, in the dry sauna. His dick so wide and thick that it hurt to jam it in. But I wanted the pain and oblivion of it. Almost bemused in the tiny cubicle, he leaned back against the flimsy wall and watched me struggle with his pole — squatting awkwardly until the massiveness took me in.

Sex, death. My body was in flames.

Shortly after, I was moving out of George's place and went down to the underground parking lot for some books. In the windshield was a note that read, "Beautiful, sex, man." Third time in a week. I looked about, but the place was deserted. Maybe it was for George? From George?

Back at the elevator I passed the Indian-looking fella in his twenties who was cleaning some glass doors.

All of a sudden, I heard "Beautiful, sex, man." It was his voice. This young, bearded janitor was the writer!

The rest is history. Or myth.

Idelmar turned out to be Brazilian. From the Amazon. An oceanography student with wonky grammar. He also turned up at my Little Italy apartment that night. I owned a bed, a kitchen table, and an Ikea starter-kit. At the front door, Idelmar held up a bottle of red wine and a couple of glasses.

I nigh on fell into his grin.

Rather like identity itself, a relationship is always at least partly defined by what it is not. For Judith Butler, the American queer theorist of note, identity is founded upon a radical lack. Just as Jacques Lacan pinpointed the reasons for our need of symbolic substitutes, Butler goes on to define the "self" as something that has suffered separation and loss: " . . . a loss which is suspended and provisionally resolved through a melancholic incorporation of some "Other." That 'Other' installed in the self thus establishes the permanent incapacity of the 'self' to achieve self-identity; it is as if we were always disrupted by the Other; the disruption

ESSAYS ON QUEER DESIRE AND SEXUALITY

of the Other at the heart of the self is the very condition of the self's possibility."

With magnolia/promiscuity, one kind of behaviour is also—and always—disrupted by its *other*. At the heart of any relationship, promiscuity wrestles with magnolia and, à la Butler, makes a fertile way ahead that destabilizes any fixed notion of how a relationship should be constructed. Just as cross-dressing upsets fixed, generally accepted views of gender and sexuality, so do innovative constructions of relationship that express the varied needs and desires of those who live them.

Judith Butler has suggested that we parody power and make fun of it in liberating acts. Monogamy, non-monogamy and promiscuity were terms handed down to us—meanings and instructions for compliance enshrined therein. It's our responsibility to send them up; and the hopeless, anachronistic behaviours they demand. As another queer theorist Judith Halberstram has pointed out, we're in a war with fixed categorizations of the "phallogocentric" centre. We need "new sexual vocabularies that acknowledge sexualities and genders as styles rather than life styles, as fictions rather than facts of life and as potentialities rather than as fixed identities."

We all negotiate passages through magnolia, promiscuity and in-between; finding a script and practice that acknowledge the past and give voice to an indefinite way ahead. In so doing we scramble David's contention that love and sexual jealous—however we might define them—destroy everything, including relationships.

It's quite the opposite, really.

We're in this wayward, unfixed discourse *because* we love and are jealous. In the queerest of antics, we take our bearings and work out radical critiques of ourselves, and society: with a view to building relationships that are sustainable, alive and pleasurable. As AIDS activist Jim Eigo said when promoting safer sex and refuting calls for monogamy by the likes of Signorile and Gabriel Rotello *(Sexual Ecology)*, "monogamy may be simpler than the dirty work of the real world, but the latter messy complexity has one significant advantage: it has a chance of being effective."

By all means magnolia or promiscuity, therefore. Purgatory has erased the rest.

65

THE LOVE THAT DARE NOT SPEAK ITS NAME

In many respects Idelmar was a lot of what I wasn't looking for: too young and too much work language-wise, for a start. I was 43; he 26. In fact, I wasn't looking at all. Was he a gigolo, an opportunist or a romantic dreamer? If so, what did that make me? Four years later we are still living together; doubts aside. Call us fantasists, lazy queers, deluded conformists — name your figure — but we've not (yet) sought out sex partners beyond the relationship, free as we are to do so. Are we drifting? Or is it like that Keatsian "negative capability" thing: "no irritable searching after fact or reason . . . ?" We make jokes about tricking and our non-existent lovers. Maybe we've regressed into something trite.

Who gives a fuck? As time passes, we may want that piece of ass outside our coupledom. And that's OK.

Whatever's kept me gnawing at the bone of "monogamy," even more than magnolia — as a baby given-up for adoption; Marjorie and Mark's fifty-year marriage as "model" (please!); my insecurities as an immigrant; a destabilized history; early poverty; foolish romanticism; search for birth-parents — there are many likely reasons for it, as there are for Idelmar: 'post'-AIDS generation, erratic parenting, virgin until he was twenty-five, sentimentality.

You name it.

Idelmar and I are not complacent or smug about these arrangements but we do seem to be content. It's a love that's everything about what suits us right now. Shaky foundation? Possibly. Journey without maps? Or future? Maybe. An act of desperation? Burnout? Opportunism? Compromise? Failure of imagination? Of courage? Blah, blah, blah . . . . Theories and story forever running alongside, like some limey wanker with his dick hanging out — congruencies, dissonances.

By accident or design we all choose our own version of a satisfying relationship. A rapport so ludicrous, it has us wondering. Part fiction, part fact. Something that commands most of our attention: most of the time. How do we possibly live it?

Without trying too hard is my guess.

Visibility
MICHAEL V. SMITH

Over the last couple years, I've been turning my sex life into a porn 'zine called *Cruising*. I've made three issues: "The Park," "Bathrooms" and "Peep Shows." The 'zine is an insider's look at public sex, with a how-to section, questionnaires, cartoons, an 'endpage' for readers to send in pics of their butt, and poems and stories, both true and imaginary, of sexual encounters in public spaces. Also, there are graphic photo essays of my drag persona, Miss Cookie LaWhore, engaged in three-ways under the stars, furtively pulling on dick under a washroom stall and swapping blowjobs with a boy in a cramped peep show booth. My favourite pic is the full-body shot of Miss Cookie standing at a washroom's trough-like urinal, with her short-shorts undone, squeezing her erection.

Because I produce this kind of confessional art, an art that graphically details a sex culture many men engage in but few discuss, a lot of people think I'm comfortable in my skin. They call me up and ask me to do glossy mag photo shoots to promote a new type of clothing for the penis. When I tell them that, given my attitude to my body in the very recent past, I consider myself to be the last person they should call. They think I'm kidding. What most people don't understand is that I don't do this nudist and graphic sex work because it's easy. I do it because exposing the nitty-gritty of my sexuality scares the shit out of me.

For years when I was younger, I tried hard, rather unsuccessfully, to disappear, to fit in. When I entered puberty, the sense of difference I felt from the other boys went from being a big secret buried in my thoughts to hard evidence, literally. Erections hit at the worst times whenever boys were around: playing in the grass, being tackled, in the locker room, the bathroom, standing in front of the class. I felt betrayed by my body, which quickly translated into distrust. The shame of being attracted to men and the fear of being found out made desire a trap.

Worse still, in my mid-teens, acne hit. I suffered with acute acne on

THE LOVE THAT DARE NOT SPEAK ITS NAME

my back for ten years because I refused to go to the doctor. I didn't want him to see me shirtless. Nobody saw me shirtless, let alone naked. If I accidentally hit an inflammation, I was in severe pain, nearly to the point of passing out, but I told no one. Compound the shame for my desire with my bloodied back, with the sense that my body was a cage, and you can see how I longed for invisibility. If you don't have a body, or if you make yourself so bland that no one notices you, people won't know a thing about you.

You might say that making a porn 'zine showing my naked dick in someone's mouth is overcompensating. Sure, my 'zine makes my sex life and my physicality visible, forcing me to be more comfortable in my skin, but really, is it necessary to share that content with the world?

In *Times Square Red Times Square Blue*, academic and sci-fi writer Samuel Delaney gives a detailed report on his decades of sex in porn houses. He uses his sexual escapades to argue that the new Times Square that has been "cleaned up" by the city is likely to prove more harmful to the American people than the community that was booted out to make way for bigger business. He argues that relocating the porn houses and prostitutes to the underpopulated harbor district displaces an established, organic and partially self-policing community that leaves them less visible and more vulnerable to violence. Less visible, more vulnerable.

That's how it works, doesn't it? A decade ago, in the midst of the AIDS crisis and its pathetic lack of funding, the queer community understood the risk involved in remaining anonymous and unheard, so much so that we used Silence = Death as our slogan.

After moving to the big city, I quickly joined the march in the malls chanting 'silence equals death' before kiss-ins. The discussion at the Queer Nation meetings where we planned the actions and hammered out our intentions made it clear to me that the slogan was more than just about AIDS funding. It was a way of life. We understood the danger of being invisible. If you tried to blend in, you were alone. If you made yourself visible, if you spoke up, you were united in the struggle and would survive. We would get what we needed only if we were vocal about those needs.

Delaney describes his public sex as building community with

ESSAYS ON QUEER DESIRE AND SEXUALITY

strangers, where you care for people who you don't know; where you are intimate with people who you know little or nothing about. It's an attitude that can change the world: to care for strangers. The proof of his argument, I believe, is in the details. I recognized in Delaney's candid report something of that necessity to tell it right, to do yourself justice by being open and honest about who you are and how you live your life. When we make the unknown familiar, the fear enveloping our sexuality falls away.

Circulating a magazine with my erect dick in it was, in part, an attempt to demystify my sexual body. I wanted to expose it to purge my fear of being seen. I wanted to make my erection familiar to address our culture's fear of sex. See me. I'm aroused. Big deal.

It's when we remove sex from the everyday, when we silence our sexuality, when we talk around our erotic life, that sex becomes perverted. In filmmaker Catherine Breillat's feature film *Romance*, two grown adults did on screen what was reserved for and isolated to the porn industry: they fucked. When I saw the film, although the penetration caught my eye, that wasn't what held my attention. It wasn't the "who-what-when and where" but the "how" and the "why" that were interesting. The way the man and woman interacted, the conversation, the manipulation, their disconnection and understanding were what kept me engaged.

Sex in the narrative. Sex as part of the storyline to further the plot and to reveal and develop character. Sex as a natural part of the story-telling because it's a natural part of our lives. Sex in the public realm.

My 'zine is an attempt to integrate my sexuality into the narrative of who I am. Queer people have been doing so as part of their personal politics for years, talking about their sexuality, expressing it publicly, putting it out there in the world, making queer sex visible to undo our collective fear.

The truth is, regardless of where you learn it, pretty much everyone is taught at a young age to fear being gay. It's *the* schoolyard taunt. For those of us who are gay, it's not "the other" that we're taught to fear, but ourselves. Fear of one's self. That's got to mess anyone up. We should pat ourselves on the back for doing a damn good job of overcoming the social stigma of being cocksuckers and fudge-packers. Against the

69

THE LOVE THAT DARE NOT SPEAK ITS NAME

greater culture's conservatism, we've come out and demanded to be counted as equals, regardless of what we do behind closed doors.

I'd like to argue, though, that most of us never lose that particular fear of being "gay." It hides, mutates or buries itself in gender. In our great sexually liberated movement, we may be proud to say who we have sex with, but we're still ashamed to be "faggy," to be "femmey," to be "feminine." Straight-looking/straight-acting has become a mantra. Since the day we sensed we were round in a square world, we've been performing in the hopes of fitting in. Straight acting. No one says they're gay-acting. Why? Because we are gay, and for whatever softness that conjures up, whatever sensitivity or sensibility it represents, that's who we are, naturally. It's why we can spot a fag from blocks away and why we recognize them even with wives on their arms.

I weigh 135 pounds. I'm over 6 feet tall. Even when I'm all butched-up in cargo pants and a plaid shirt, men drive by in their cars and yell "faggot" at me. There's no hiding what I am. "Queerness" falls off my body like pearls. And I love it.

I don't want to debate whether or not there is an "essential" gayness out there, but there's a sensitivity to the world, an understanding of the arbitrariness, the double standard, the falseness of the common cultural myth of what it is to be a "man" that any fag who has come out must have grappled with at some point. Fags are men. Like it or not, the quee-niest guy in the world is a still a guy, and therefore the definition of what it means to be a "man" has to be broad enough to encompass him.

When you look at it that way, when you consider all the different types of men out there, it becomes a lot harder to say what a man is. We're cheating ourselves out of a great gift if we bury that insight under a false identity, an act, for the sake of blending in. The gift is diversity, a valuable equalizer that's been forgotten in our struggle to find commonality.

The more I explore my girlishness, the more powerful I feel. Being femme isn't emasculating. Throw on a skirt one day, gentlemen, and see how much power you need to draw on to walk down the street. The days I dress femme challenge me not to buy into the narrow cultural definitions of what I'm expected to be. I'm my own type of person, which is less and less prescribed every day.

70

ESSAYS ON QUEER DESIRE AND SEXUALITY

When I finally admitted to the world that I was gay, it was such a relief to be able to throw off the burden of what a straight guy was expected to be. I wasn't just seeking the freedom to do in the bedroom what I wanted and with whom. I was after the celebration of my whole self, the whole complex person I had hidden away in there. The biggest bonus for me in coming out was that it meant I could abandon the prescribed rules and rituals of being "a man." If I felt like it, I could wear pink. I could be tender in public. I could cry at movies. Paint my nails. Read Paglia. I could jump for joy on the street corner. Kiss men hello. Use colorful adjectives. Be polite. Admit my fears in public. Be kind and sensitive.

There's nothing stopping straight men from any of those things, except a cultural myth that men are one thing and women another. We like to think that males and females vary in their body makeup, but we ignore the transgendered and the intersexed who defy the categories of the binary system. The saying holds: people are people. Regardless of our reductive gender labels, we all share the human experience. So fags should use the freedom to be who they are, which includes being feminine, so that, like everything else fashionable that eventually makes it into the culture of masculinity, that too will be embraced.

Queers are the gender educators of this world. We've learned the hard way what it is to grow up different, to see the world of black and white in colors. We know the cultural stereotypes and their limitations, the contradiction, the arbitrary nature of a defined manhood. We didn't fit in when we were children, so why try now? The goal, as I see it, is to continue to not fit until there are so many of us that the gendered walls fall, making room for everyone.

71

Confessions

EMANUEL XAVIER

When I was about three years old, we lived in Coney Island. I was forced to share a bed with my teenage cousin, Lucho. For over a year, he would molest me, just about every other night, in every way unimaginable. I am a survivor of sexual abuse.

Though I had no control over my first experiences, I have been in touch with my sexuality ever since. Negative repercussions aside, somewhere along the way, I realized I could get what I wanted if I was extra-special super-charming. Crying only made things worse. Tantrums got me nowhere. Loud, exaggerated laughter and fluttering eyelashes always got me candy. I was one of those spoiled brats that could get away with anything. I was inappropriately flirtatious with adults throughout my adolescence. During family visits, I would make my uncles uncomfortable by sitting or resting my head suggestively on their laps.

As a child, I spent every summer vacation in Ecuador. By the age of eleven, I was teaching an older cousin how to masturbate. We would share a bed after watching soft porn on late-night South American television, and I would simply spit on my hand and jerk off next to him. I encouraged him to take my lead and, soon enough, he was shooting his load all over me every night. Eventually, I would pretend to be asleep as he dry humped me from the side. One night, I conveniently helped him maneuver his dick inside of me. Needless to say, we moved on from mutual masturbation and went straight to fucking every night. Of course, I was fast asleep through it all and remember nothing to this day (insert wicked smile here). My moaning was just a result of recurring nightmares.

I would look forward to our annual travel plans until one year he decided we should stop fucking around before I "turned gay." I remember being completely confused, especially after he started going out with

ESSAYS ON QUEER DESIRE AND SEXUALITY

the little slut across the street. I was reduced to an occasional quickie whenever the bitch was giving him a hard time. He started wrestling with some serious demons about his sexuality, and it wasn't long before I got bored with him completely.

When puberty officially hit, my ass once again became the object of much attention. I had developed a big butt and it didn't help much that I was being teased in school. I had definitely inherited this asset from my mother. I used to hate walking down the streets of Brooklyn with her and having men catcall, whistle and make rude comments to the woman next to me in daisy dukes. She apparently enjoyed the attention. I was totally embarrassed that my mother was the object of such desire. I didn't like my friends thinking my mother was such a hottie.

Soon enough, I realized gay men were staring at my own ass on the subway. Tight blue jeans probably didn't help much. Like most teens, contradiction of my own true self was the only way possible to become aware of who I was and what I wanted in life. It seemed pretty dreadful until I was out on the streets and learned I could make money off of it.

By the time I hit the West Side Highway piers, there was no doubt that my butt was my greatest feature. When my mother found out I was gay and put my ass out on the streets, it was my saving grace. It didn't take long before someone was offering me money and a place to spend the night. At sixteen, rebellious and sexually charged, I took to hustling with a vengeance.

It also helped that I was simultaneously cursed and blessed with a younger appearance. Though I was already underage, the fact that I could pass for twelve helped me keep an edge over the competition. To this day, I've been known to milk the whole "young Latino boy" image. I never met my real father, which probably explains why I had no problem working through a series of daddies.

When I was hustling, I had a variety of experiences ranging from the conventional to the esoteric. I admit that I sometimes found myself in unwanted positions, but there were important lessons I learned along the way. Though, at such a crucial age, it was a decadent way to explore my own sexuality, I discovered many things about myself.

For one, I get really turned on by making out. There is something passionate and private about two people kissing. It was the perfect con-

73

THE LOVE THAT DARE NOT SPEAK ITS NAME

quest, especially because it was so taboo with many tricks and most of the other hustlers. It was frustrating because it seemed like the greatest contradiction. Sex was perfectly OK, but exchanging saliva was personal. Like it would make a difference to their boyfriends or wives whether they made out with a hustler or not after having sex with one. It's like anyone who still believes giving head is not really sex because there is no penetration involved. I may have been a prostitute, but at least I was honest with myself about who I was and what I was doing.

Today, this all manifests into my current relationships because I've learned that sex can be mechanical for some people, but a kiss is so revealing. It distinguishes the difference between making love and just having sex. I can shamelessly admit that I'm a good kisser. I *know* that because I've been told so many times. It validates the warmth I offer during sex. I love the wetness of a kiss with tongues dancing, especially when it is hungry and intense.

I also caught on during my hustling days that I enjoy giving head more than getting it. I enjoy the taste of a good cock. In fact, I only eat poultry and fish, so it is the only meat I eat. It would take days for someone to get me to cum by blowing me. I think that has more to do with control than anything else. However, I've always been complimented for my lip service.

I've always enjoyed looking up at the person I am sucking off and making eye contact. Words left unspoken are incredibly sexy. I find sex talk absurd when so much can be expressed with a simple touch or just the right grunt.

Altoids were my favorite mints for expanding the throat muscles until discovering Listermints. There is something to be said about going down on a man with fresh breath and leaving their cocks raw with menthol. I'm not particularly affectionate toward the taste of cum, so I usually pop one in following sex to kill the aftertaste. Unless, of course, I get pulled up to make out with a mouth full of cum, which is always a thrill.

After having been with so many different types of men, I know that the one physical thing that really excites me would have to be his chest. I have a preference toward those that are hairy. I suppose it's because I have a smooth chest that compliments one very well. I've been trying for years now to grow hair on my chest to no avail. There's something

ESSAYS ON QUEER DESIRE AND SEXUALITY

unruly and arousing about a little fur. And it's even hotter when a man trims his chest and the spiky hair gently scratches against your face while sucking on a nipple.

My favorite foreplay has always been getting eaten out. While hustling, I didn't have much choice in the matter. Nowadays, however, I've become such a control freak, and I must feel completely comfortable; nonetheless, once it's offered, they can go at it for days like all-you-can-eat sushi.

I usually want to get fucked after being toyed with. Size really doesn't matter as long as it is maneuvered properly. Oversized cocks look great and are tempting but are simply too painful, and unusually small dicks are just frustrating because they never really fulfill. I'm also scared off by unusual curves that could land someone in the emergency room.

Though I have only had sex with a handful of women, I have enjoyed getting fucked with a dildo by a butch lesbian. I've met some sexy butches that really turn me on. I suppose it has to do with their masculinity and aggressive nature. I think every gay man should get fucked by a strap-on dyke at least once in their lives (insert another wicked smile here). It would make for a more unified community.

With time, I've realized that some tops have a problem with me because they want to be the aggressors. It's all about control. Sex is equated with power. It's confusing for some tops to have an aggressive bottom that calls the shots. It's difficult for a bottom to have that power and remain sexy at the same time. Once they realize I'm headstrong, independent and smart, they become insecure and go limp.

They want me to be that child and hustler who had no choice but to be completely submissive. I guess it was when I started having recreational sex that I began to say "no" when I felt I was being hurt, or I when was simply not ready.

The flipside to that would be sex with a partner who is aware of your past and takes extra care not to harm you. Courtesy and sensitivity during sex do not turn me on. There is no way to get elegantly fucked. It is not unusual for survivors of sexual abuse to find eroticism in a little pleasurable pain or playful violence. Sex between consenting adults should be raw and unapologetic.

I am most comfortable as a bottom, but I do have moments when I

THE LOVE THAT DARE NOT SPEAK ITS NAME

need to fuck someone. Within a relationship, I think it is most practical to be versatile. It balances off power and breaks down sexual boundaries. There is nothing more exhilarating than being able to fuck the man that constantly provides you with great pleasure himself. However, I have been in relationships where we both needed a "husband" since we were both "bottoms." These relationships were particularly frustrating because we both wanted desperately to get fucked by the other.

After all of my experiences, I realize that the sexiest thing about any man for me would have to be his brain. Intelligence is stimulating. I'm attracted to many different types of men, ranging from all backgrounds and physical aspects, but if I can't have an interesting conversation with him, it's not going anywhere beyond the bedroom. I have to admit that speaking English is important to me because it is how I naturally communicate. As an American Latino, or Americano, I think and dream in English and have to translate the words in my mind before verbalizing complete Spanish phrases. I can deal with a little Spanish during sex for nostalgia, but anything more becomes annoying.

I am also keen on spiritual men. I am religious in the broadest sense of the word. I light candles occasionally and say my prayers, and am always aware that God is watching. I was raised Catholic, but I have an interest in all religions. Passion, sexuality and religion all bleed into each other for me. I think you can be simultaneously sexual and religious and spiritual at the same time.

Surviving life on the streets as a hustler taught me to be open-minded about sexuality. Some people still have this idea that if a gay man is sexually active, they're not happy and healthy. I, myself, have been a victim of many interesting rumors. My favorite is that I didn't lose a few pounds by working out and dieting because I wanted to, but because I'm dying of HIV-related symptoms. The response has always been quite simple: Condoms are not an interruption to me unless there isn't one available. They've saved my life.

Of course, there are still those people, who, no matter what I do, will always think of me as a prostitute. Everybody has their image that precedes them. My sexual image is looming out there in front of me. Everyone probably thinks that I'm just a raving nymphomaniac, that I have an insatiable sexual appetite, when the truth is I'd rather be read-

ESSAYS ON QUEER DESIRE AND SEXUALITY

ing a book. I feel sexually fulfilled at this point in my life, and not as restless as I used to be.

I find that dating after thirty sucks because most everyone has already experienced a bad relationship. You have to put up with the demons that both of you carry around. I've been involved with one-too-many serious drug addicts and young boys that have had a lot of growing up to do. It is extremely rare when two individuals are instinctively drawn to each other, and are at the same place in their lives.

In essence, I believe sexuality—your own sexual identity—is crucial. The more you pay attention to it, the more you understand that just about everything in the world is centered around sexual attraction and power.

There are great contradictions about love in that it is something very powerful yet remarkably fragile. In retrospect, I can honestly say that I've been lucky enough to have been in love and been loved. I am a hopeless romantic. And I have great faith in love.

Seals

MATT BERNSTEIN SYCAMORE

Wednesday, July 10, 2002

I want to think about how when I look at you it's so much beauty, how lying on top of you is just calm. I want to think about holding and holding and HOLDING you. Sure, I'm ignoring all those weird smells of smoke and sweat and other rotten things—or even inhaling all of that, you—and letting it sit inside. I want to think about knowing you for ten years—bitch, that's a long time. I was nineteen when I met you and I was so old, struggling, sure, but bold. You were so much of everything I wanted to be, you were always breaking but making so much. I don't want this to be a poem; I want to hold you until you heal. I'm glad we can laugh about it, everything, and still feel. I'm glad that when you say, *sure, a terrorist attack would be a bad thing, but I don't really care*—I know that you mean there's so much of everything wrong in every little fucking corner of the goddamn world and especially in this sickening monster of a country, and how are we supposed to survive, even thrive—without diving off? I want to sit in a steam room until I pass out. I want to throw bricks through windows, bombs in basements—but I'm scared of what they'd do to me, to us. What they already do to us, before we even have a chance to scream HELP! HELP! HELP!

You said you'd tested positive and I'd already cried on the bus about the possibility 'cause you'd asked for help and I can't remember the last time. For a second I just wanted to get FUCKED, come in my ass until I passed out from the danger. I looked at your eyes, so much softness and yearning. All that glassy sassy green and why did I look away? Sure, we hugged and petted and kissed and caressed and it was so, so much beauty, but maybe we could have cried, died—that's not the word I was looking for—we both know how to swim, and besides, bodies float in salt water anyway.

Tuesday, July 16, 2002

Rue said he hasn't really cried yet, wishes he could and I thought about giving him what I wrote last week but I was scared. He said, *I've just been so busy, all the appointments.* Decided he's not gonna drink or do drugs at all. He said, *It just doesn't make sense when the alcohol and the meds were so much a part of what got me to where I am. I mean, I take full responsibility, but there were just all those nights when I blacked out and found myself wandering home at six a.m., no idea what I'd just done.*

Rue said, *I think the meds might really have made the difference* — maybe that's why I stayed negative for so long, cause I wasn't on any meds. I'm glad she brought up the meds because that way I could talk about them. I said, *Honey, you were scary when you were on the highest dosage. I thought it was the meds but then I just thought maybe you were becoming scary* — I didn't want to take away your right to choose. But then your dosage went down and I thought, good, she's back. But the first thing your therapist does is say, *Here's a higher dose of these pills so we can get rid of your immunity, and here are some of these pills so you can go party.* We laughed about that together.

I showed him what I wrote last week, kissed his ears and his forehead while he read it. He finished and started sobbing softly, tears running down his face and I was kissing them. It felt romantic. Maybe that's the wrong word. Soulful? He said, *Sometimes I just wish I could spit it all out, all the horrible things in this world. I've been so neurotic about my health. I take like thirty pills every morning and I've been eating really well. I've just been so stressed out. I need to find what's gonna give me the most meaning and I'm just not sure.*

Tuesday, July 23, 2002

I woke up on Sunday to a message from Tony saying, *I can't wait to see you.* It made me so happy. Went over to meet him in the East Bay and we ate at Cha-ya, then over to his house to lie in bed because he was tired from doing K all weekend. It just felt so great lying there with him, especially hugging him from behind which is the way he likes it, even if it makes my shoulder hurt. I wanted someone to come in and snap a

THE LOVE THAT DARE NOT SPEAK ITS NAME

photo; we were so cute. Went to Aquatic Park to have sex because Sarah was home. I wanted to have sex in the apartment anyway, but I guess there is only that sheet separating Tony's bed from the rest of the apartment—and Aquatic Park sounded good anyway. Tony was fucking my face and I started bleeding. He wiped it off with his underwear, which was so cute, held my face and said, *Are you OK?*

We walked out on this dock to a pagoda and etched M + T into the railing because Mattilda + Tony was too hard to write. A woman was walking her dog as the sun was going down and the fags started arriving. Tony said, *Does she know what goes on in this park?* We went behind a few bushes and Tony got on his knees. I wondered why I still get nervous before sex—it's been seven months and I still have some weird performance anxiety—probably from being a whore for so long. First thing in my head is, *Am I gonna get hard?* The mosquitoes started biting my legs while Tony was sucking my cock—which he's become an expert at, the seven months really helps there—then holding me from behind while I shot deep into the trees and the woman threw a ball for her dog with one of those ball-throwers and a few guys sort-of watched. Tony hugged me and said, *I love you,* and it was so sweet. I always resist saying I love you after sex 'cause I'm thinking that's cheesy, but it's weird to resist. It's not some random person, it's beautiful, beautiful Tony who I love more and more. It makes me giddy just to be with him. I feel lighter, more childlike and possibly even free, not to sound like Jean-Paul Sartre or anything, but really. Tony went home to watch *Frontier Life* where everyone pretends they're on the frontier, and I joked about it.

Woke up yesterday from a dream where Tony wanted to die and then he did, just from willing it, and when I woke up I was scared, even though I knew it was just superstition. I called him anyway and left a message. Then I got all hypoglycemic and worried about losing him, which happens so fast, my stomach clenches up and I feel nauseous. What if he met someone else? I know it's stupid but I can't help feeling it.

Went out to dinner with Jenna, which was fun. I was explaining Tony to her—after eight years of not being involved in a sexual relationship, and how easy this one is, how sweet and romantic. It just seems right, really—like why on earth would it end? How we have our own

80

ESSAYS ON QUEER DESIRE AND SEXUALITY

lives and that's good; we have our own life together and that's good, too. How sometimes I get all freaked out about our differences, like is it just too much, but that's always when we're apart—when do those fucking moments stop? I guess when I actually start sleeping well and feeling good.

Today I went to therapy and of course I was so fucking exhausted and through with it, with feeling this way when I've tried every way not to. I closed my eyes and pictured the exhaustion, my skeleton with blood and guts everywhere, standing in front of me with huge fangs, ready to cut out my heart and eat it. Karen said, *What do you want it to do?* I let it eat my heart and then I was dead, a skeleton on the ground with bugs and people stepping on it, cracking my ribs. Even though I was dead, that still hurt. Then there was a part of me floating away in a flower basket: seals in a pool, but that pool's not big enough for seals. Mountains and lakes for the seals—and I was playing with them. It was so much fun.

Then people came and killed the seals for their fur. I kept seeing the image from the D.C. zoo, of seals cut open and their bellies filled with the pennies people threw in the water. People are stupid, or evil—that's what I was thinking. And how did we get to the part where Karen was asking the repetitive question: first it was, *What makes you exhausted?* My father, my mother, my sister, being exhausted, sleep, sadness, anger, there were more specific things too but I can't remember. Then Karen asked, *What makes you happy?* First it was my writing but now that hurts because of my fucking tendonitis. It used to work, though. Then we got to Tony, petting me and holding me in his lap. Oh, I feel so much lighter, my body in his arms feels different, more relaxed. Karen said, *Is that relaxation different from the exhaustion,* which was a smart question and yes, it was so, so different, all this energy radiating out of my body and upwards too and I was the center of it all. Then Rue was next to me; all that love in his eyes, and Tony and Rue were hugging me. Oh, it was so beautiful and safe.

Then came the bad part. Karen said, *How is this different from your father?* Oh, it was scary. I got so triggered, so frightened that it would be my father, and how could I ever separate all this beauty from all that darkness? Would I ever feel that beauty again? Would it ever be safe? My

THE LOVE THAT DARE NOT SPEAK ITS NAME

head started pounding right in between my eyebrows and I was hitting my face and biting my hands out of desperation. I felt so angry at Karen. How could she ruin that beautiful state? How could she bring my father into that safe space; finally, a safe space and now my father was looming over it, his eyes, the axe through my body, nothing but pain and sadness and death inside.

I felt so cold, shut off and angry and desperate and despondent. Cold like I made myself in my father's house in order to survive, but now that's the scariest feeling possible, like I'm never going to escape the despair, like I have to be dead inside in order to stay alive. I was trying to cry but I couldn't, everything was stuck inside. When I left I was so fucking exhausted, rushed home to lie in bed instead of going to yoga. No, I needed to rest. Then I called Tony and that was such a good idea. At first I was afraid to tell him the whole story, but afterwards I felt so much better and no longer desperate, more alive and still tired, sure, but good enough to get groceries and come home and relax.

Sunday, July 28, 12:22 a.m.

I can't believe I made the mistake of going to the Dore Alley Street Fair. On our way there, this circuit monster was having a seizure from I-don't-know-what scary drug combination. His friends were holding him up against a wall while another friend ran away to party some more. They were all so tan and buff and tweaked out, and I was worried the guy was going to die but I didn't know what to do to help. My mood was so low. I kept saying, *I need to go home and commit suicide.* I live in San Francisco so that I don't have to interact with these people; it's so fucking depressing how gay people are. Ralowe said, *This is more embarrassing than going to see any Stephen Spielberg movie,* 'cause I'm always making fun of him for that.

I rushed home in a cab, tore off my clothes because really I felt dirty, literally, and Tony arrived just as I was getting dressed. I was sketchy. We got in bed and it actually worked, just resting my hand on his hip made me so calm. Even though it fucked up my shoulder because of the angle. Every time he touches me, I feel so much love moving in and out. He came all over my face and snapped some photos, then I showed him how I used to jerk off by pumping the sink top like I was fucking—only now I discovered that I can use my kitchen counter. Grabbed some olive oil for lube, and when I shot, I came in a big pile. Hugged Tony in so many different ways, like my head in his lap, kissing his toes, or behind him, lying on my side with my arm underneath his head and around to his chest. I get so excited just to be with him—light rising out of my eyes and rejuvenating me.

Saturday, August 17, 2002

Friday was my day to hang out with Tony between my trip and his trip. I went over to his new apartment and he was kinda manic but happy. He kept saying, *I could live here for the rest of my life.* It was so relaxing holding hands and just looking at him. I took him out to Millenium, where the woman next to us said to her friend: *We meet in the most exotic places. Remember Uruguay?* But the food was amazing, so fun to eat slowly and taste all the complicated flavors. And share that with someone—Tony—who I love. He was excited too and we savored that. Then we went back to his house for a nap but ending up having sex—surprise—he came all over my face, yum, too bad no camera. Then he collapsed in the bed and I was still horny, grinding against him. *Is this OK?* He said, *Yeah, it's lulling me to sleep.* I was hugging him and grinding really slowly, savoring the pressure on the top of my dick and the build-up until I couldn't take it any more. I was groaning louder and louder and holding tighter until the most fucking amazing orgasm. I was panting and almost shaking, a big stream of come all over Tony and my leg. He turned to kiss me and then I was so high, watching the reflection of light on the ceiling. How pretty! When Tony gave up on the nap, we talked about one of his linguistics terms—bilabial slips or was it stops? I don't know how it came up, but I think it was when two consonant sounds are different because with one you use the vocal chords and with the other you don't: mmm and nnn. We were practising them. I was joking about mmm because Tony's gay.com name is sexmmm—or something like that.

THE LOVE THAT DARE NOT SPEAK ITS NAME

Wednesday, August 21, 2002, 11:12 p.m.

OK, well, my tendons nerves muscles ACHE and burn when I sit to type
and handwriting is almost worse, but fuck it. I'm a writer dammit. I need
to write! Just now I was thinking how I've come to accept less than what
I want from almost all my friends, and that's OK if each person is fulfill-
ing a need that someone else isn't, and then it all adds up—but when it's
almost everyone giving me less than I want, and I just accept that, then
I think I might have a problem.

I guess I was thinking about Rue. How I reached this point of peace
with our relationship not meeting all of my expectations—and relaxed
about that, felt the beauty that is present and cherished it. But now I feel
like I can never predict when he'll be present, or even interested in being
present. I went to Wolf Creek mostly to hang out with him, to spend time
together outside of the city and away from the everyday pressures of our
lives. And Wolf Creek was absolutely fucking amazing. It really opened
me up to so many possibilities of human interaction and healing. But I
barely hung out with Rue at all, she was in a bitchy mood all the
time—and it was good that I found other people to love, that the land
drew me in—otherwise it would have been awful.

Obviously Rue was going through a ton—especially after she told
Wiley he'd seroconverted and Wiley flew back from Brazil to join us. So,
sure, I can excuse her; of course I can excuse her. It's just that I feel like
I'm always just accepting and accepting and it's reaching a breaking
point. And she was such a bitch, too, not just absent and unavailable, but
truly bitchy and I guess that's what I can't really forgive. Then we had a
beautiful moment on the phone and I thought, *OK, everything's fine—I
was wrong to be stressed out*—but then the sketchiness always comes back,
like today on the phone I just sensed she wasn't present and I shut off,
immediately, 'cause I didn't really feel that she cared. Though just the
other day Ralowe said, *Seeing you two interact gives me hope in the world.*
And that's true for me, too, just gotta figure out how to build that.

Sunday, September 8, 2002

Guess I've waited a while to write about this—'cause I've talked about it

84

ESSAYS ON QUEER DESIRE AND SEXUALITY

so much—and also 'cause I was scared to be dramatic I guess. So, anyway, sometimes Tony and I have these annoying conversations that maybe he enjoys but I hate. Right when we met, he liked to have the one starting with, *All art is dead because anybody can make art.* The one from a few weeks ago started with him saying, *Ginkgo Biloba—it doesn't help your memory, study after study has proven that it doesn't work . . .* and led up to, *Natural health is really just a niche market ploy by companies to make money off of people's ignorance.* I guess the thing I like the least about these conversations is that Tony gets so angry, like my father used to, and I get drawn in. But then it's over and I know I love Tony anyway and who cares about an annoying conversation here and there.

Then we had a second one. This one's ongoing and I might have brought it on: *Is San Francisco a progressive city?* Tony argued that just because homeless people can still access benefits means San Francisco is a progressive city. I said, *That's a pretty low standard.*

After dinner, I got really tired—maybe it was because of the conversations or maybe not—and had to go home and take a nap. That's one of my favorite things to do with Tony: nap. But this time Tony didn't want to nap; he wanted to leave. I said, *I'd really like to hang out for a few more hours. Do you want to come back?* But no, he wanted to go home and then get drinks; he hadn't gone out all week. Never mind the three times he did K at home. I got really sad, caught myself changing my facial expression so he wouldn't see. I said: *I just feel really sad. You make me happier so I want to hang out for a little longer.* He left.

I took a nap. When I got up I was a DISASTER. All I could think about was drugs, could even feel the rush to my head but I was very rational about it. I knew I wanted drugs because drugs make me feel invulnerable for a few hours, but then soon enough I feel much more vulnerable. I knew I couldn't leave the house because then it would be over, I kept thinking of excuses like maybe I should just get a cocktail at the Lush Lounge because they have fresh lemon juice, even though I haven't had a cocktail in who knows how long. Instead I kept calling people: Rhani, Jason, Erica, Rue. Talked it all through and then I went to bed.

When Tony and I hang out (or with any of my good friends), sometimes right away we have that amazing closeness and sometimes it takes

THE LOVE THAT DARE NOT SPEAK ITS NAME

five hours. That day Tony and I hadn't gotten there yet and he wanted to leave before it happened, couldn't do me such a small favor of staying when I'm always waiting for his naps. And actually, I like that. Waiting makes me happy that this beautiful boy who I love is resting in my bed. When he left I just felt scared, like would he help me in an emergency if an hour was too long to wait—when he didn't have any other plans. Actually he had plans to hang out with me. Though the way he saw it was that our time was over and he just needed to go home. Which is fine, just that I asked him to stay—which was really hard, to be vulnerable like that—and then he left. Called him the next day and he said he didn't realize how important it was to me, maybe that makes sense. I thought I was clear, but who knows. I said, *Well, in the future if it happens again, will you stay?* He said, *Yes.*

So everything was fine. It's just that moments like that open up this whole list of questions for me. Because basically we have different worldviews: his is pretty much mainstream liberal/progressive, mine is outsider/freak/radical. There are people who get up in the morning, look outside the window, and think, *How on earth do I relate to that horrible place outside?* Then there are people who never ask that question. I'm in the first category, Tony's somewhere in between. Plus there's the question of whether you're at least committed to vague attempts to change the horror (internally or externally)—I'm not sure Tony is. He certainly isn't dedicated to working out issues in our relationship. He can't deal with processing at all. I have to be really creative in discussing anything. On one level, I appreciate the challenge except I'm always scared that if I bring something up the wrong way, he'll feel threatened or scared and say, *OK maybe we're just not compatible.* Like in the very beginning of our relationship, he was ready to give up because our sex wasn't immediately easy.

I can feel myself growing and loving in new ways and I see that with Tony too. I have this confidence that he'll grow more open, that our differences don't really matter because we get so much beauty and awareness from each other. I love the way he makes me feel childlike and vulnerable and happy in ways that were never safe for me as a child. Like when he saw tears in my eyes from petting a stuffed seal in the marine mammal gift shop at Pier 39, and then later he bought it for me.

ESSAYS ON QUEER DESIRE AND SEXUALITY

That made me so happy. I guess I just want to feel safer. Funny I used that word, because another thing that's really changed since we started going out is that we made a commitment not to have unprotected anal sex with anyone (else), and that's really changed my behavior—I can barely imagine it now. Before, getting fucked without a condom almost felt like foreplay.

One thing I realized is that I keep on making myself vulnerable, and sometimes I don't see him doing the same thing. I guess my fear is that I'll just open myself more and more and then eventually I'll get really hurt.

Monday, September 9, 2002, 12:07 a.m.

So Tony and I had the conversation that I was dreading, delaying, trying to avoid, etc. It started because he was smoking in the car and I got in and said, *Oh, you don't even bother to open the window when I'm not in the car.* I said it in a joking manner and even kissed him first, but he said, *It's my fucking car; I'll smoke in it if I want to.* He looked really upset and angry and full of hate. I said, *Don't talk to me like that. Is something wrong?* He said, *Maybe something is wrong.* I said, *Let's get dinner and then we can talk about it afterwards.*

I got really scared. I thought as soon as we're done with this conversation, I'm gonna do coke. Just once, I've gotta feel that high. But then we had the conversation, and now I feel much better. Even excited that maybe our relationship will grow in new ways. Funny how we were thinking about the same issues. Just a few notes: how he can't conceptualize changing the way we have sex so that our relationship can grow. By that I mean moving away from orgasm as the only destination or goal and into seeing sex as a way to experience and build intimacy and trust. Like if I get scared and want him to hold me for a while, I want to be able to say so—that's pretty basic. He thinks that's just too much work, takes away the pleasure of sex. If he's not willing to work on building trust, maybe we should move away from sex. Maybe it's healthier for me that way.

I'm just glad that we talked; maybe now I won't have to be as careful about what I say, though I completely understand what he said about

87

THE LOVE THAT DARE NOT SPEAK ITS NAME

me being too harsh about bars, etc.—have to be conscious about that. Another interesting part was talking about whether you can change because of intention—he used the word "will." My entire existence is guided by will, otherwise I'd be tearing apart the people I love as a sign of respect, and I'd be a completely coked-out mess, not to mention a thousand other horrors. The thing I'm most worried about is that he won't be as committed to me/our relationship without sex, or that "boyfriend" designation. I really value him in my life, especially as a consistent presence, and I don't want to lose that. Or the amazingly beautiful physical intimacy that feels so healing. It would be nice to commit to arriving at a deep place of connection, every time we meet. Maybe a ritual, even. I wonder if he'd think that was new-agey.

Tuesday, September 10, 2002, 2:33 a.m.

Damn I have to go to bed soon, but first some notes about the conversation. Tony wants his "emotional independence," which I would call emotional distance—he's comfortable with that and doesn't want to change or even question anything about himself in order to grow closer to me. I guess the bottom line is that my confidence (I even used the word "faith") was that he would open up to me, that he would make me feel safe. If I just kept making myself vulnerable. I wonder whether that confidence is just delusion. Tony said, *I don't want to make you vulnerable.* I said, *Vulnerable is fine—I don't want to be destroyed.* So we came to an agreement there—that we should shift the relationship into new territory that acknowledges the reality of what we offer each other.

He kept talking about transitioning from being boyfriends to being friends and I just didn't want those definitions. Later I realized that I don't want to be friends. I want to be family. I said something about talking from different cultures and how hard that is: my culture of questioning and processing everything, his culture of avoidance and moving on. Earlier he was saying he felt single when he wasn't with me—that feeling was about his lack of commitment and he was OK with that. But then what's the transition?

At one point Tony kept insisting that we needed two weeks without talking, to "start the grieving process." He kept saying we have to meet

ESSAYS ON QUEER DESIRE AND SEXUALITY

again like we've never met, but I don't like people who I've just met—especially when I know all their faults ahead of time. I got scared. What fucking grieving process? We both acknowledge that we need to shift things—why are we grieving? Can't we create a deeper, more honest relationship? I don't want to fucking grieve. That's some formula: go out, break up, grieve, become friends. Can't we transcend that—it feels artificial. I know that if Tony doesn't want to change the way we have sex, then it's not healthy for us—that's how the conversation started, with sex, that was our first agreement and then he moved on to cover the entirety of our relationship.

What I do know is that I don't want to think, *Oh, there's that bitch Tony*—or worse, feel my stomach sink and my voice get hollow. I want to walk away holding hands, like we used to—feeling connected to Tony and the beauty we share.

Friday, September 13, 2002, 12:07 a.m.

I'm so glad I have Rue in my life. Went over to his house and I was so exhausted I could hardly speak. He made dinner and then he was exhausted. We lay in his bed and petted each other. I like how easy and caring the physicality between us feels; of course, we've had ten years to work on it. Then he went to sleep and I sat in the kitchen, finally calm and not wanting to leave.

Back to Tony—number one, he feels that sex for him is always best the first time, then it gets progressively worse. Sex for him is that aggressive, charged, orgasm-focused activity that's all drive until the comeshot and then it's nap-time. Maybe I should have paid more attention to the first time we had sex—which was beautiful and hot—but at the height of it he was trying over and over again to slide his dick into my ass without a condom (and without asking). Later, when I confronted him about that, he agreed that it was good I kept angling away—of course it was *my* responsibility to keep safe, his responsibility was only to his pleasure (one reason why so many fags are still seroconverting, tops who won't take responsibility).

I could go on but let's get back to Tony. He isn't interested in seeing sex as something you work at—of course that's why our sex hasn't got-

THE LOVE THAT DARE NOT SPEAK ITS NAME

ten better, because he can't talk about it. Sex with someone I love is an opening into a new world of trust and shared intimacy. Tony doesn't want that, he doesn't want to hold me when I feel triggered or lie in bed petting me for two hours. That isn't *sex*. I guess he just wants to pump me full of come; he wants sex (and everything) to be easy all the time (he said that)—I don't even know what that means. I've really never experienced *anything* as easy. It means *on his own terms:* Whiteboy Syndrome. Did I mention the fucked-up gender dynamic? He thinks that of course I deserve someone who will hold me when I'm triggered, but he's not interested in going there. I think he sees it as a hard/soft thing (once again, he's the man and I'm the woman), but I guess he forgets that the first thing he couldn't do was smack my chest or spit on me.

Number two goes a bit deeper. Tony feels comfortable with "emotional independence." His emotional independence is what keeps him happy, and he imagines that at some point in the future he may change, but for now that's what he wants. He isn't interested in feeling emotionally committed to me, or any lover. It's my worst fear—that I'll keep making myself vulnerable, with the hope that eventually he'll open up. But it'll never happen. I guess I appreciate his honesty but it doesn't make any thing easy.

I recognize that with these insights, our relationship needs to change. I just don't want to lose the beauty. I want to lie in his arms and appreciate the texture of his hands, his lips. I want to feel that childlike vulnerability and happiness. I don't need the distance that Tony thinks is necessary. I want to move into a new relationship that recognizes the truth and creates a more sustained intimacy. I'm just scared that he wants to shut me out in order to feel safe. He's motivated so much by his fears. He kept talking about drifting back into what we're used to—that's about his previous relationships. None of it is about me, *my* fears. I'm not a fucking piece of driftwood; when I make a decision it's made. But Tony doesn't believe in will.

On Tuesday, I had the most amazing therapy session. It was right after my most recent conversation with Tony, and I arrived feeling so sad. Closed my eyes and I was back to two-years-old, looking at my sister. She's so cute but so scared. She doesn't like being naked; they do things to her when she's naked. They do things to me too, but I'm older.

ESSAYS ON QUEER DESIRE AND SEXUALITY

Though not much older. Then I was looking at all the cute seals that are killed for mink coats and the lobsters people boil alive, etc. and then all the little kids on busses who aren't protected and you can see it 'cause their eyes are rolled back, and everyone knows and no one does anything. Then I was crying for all these little kids; I mean bawling like I hadn't done in months or maybe even years. Crying for all the kids who aren't protected—no one protected me—and what can be done for all these kids? I felt so sad and helpless. I hated humans so much. I was crying and crying because what could I possibly do? When I left the office, I didn't quite feel hopeful but I felt more like myself.

Monday, September 16, 2002, 1:06 a.m.

I thought I'd end this piece nice and tidy and sad, sad, SAD, but I guess maybe there's more. Dinner with Tony next week, just dinner. We're only allowed to have dinner. I said, *I want to make sure that you're committed to feeling close and not distant.* He wouldn't commit, just said, *That would be nice.* He said that obviously he felt the same way I do, the same sadness. I said, *Well, you've never told me that, so no, I had no idea.* Tony said, *You're just being*—what was his word—not manipulative, what was it? Oh, he said, *You're just rationalizing.* How condescending—I want to build a beautiful relationship and he calls that rationalizing. Dare to dream, bitch—dare to fucking dream!

Wednesday, September 18, 2002, 6:35 p.m.

This morning—at one of the points when I woke up too early—I had the realization that Tony wants to start our new relationship on the same terms as the old. *His* terms, of course. I realize that my hope that he might share his feelings is probably a delusion. I don't think that's what he wants. He wants to meet without tension or strife—or hope? I just feel like, where is the potential for growth, where is the potential for me to receive any sort of support? I'm worried about two possibilities: 1) that I'll give in to all his terms, continuing under the same fear/lack of direct communication scheme, or 2) I'll insist that he meet me somewhere and he'll refuse.

91

THE LOVE THAT DARE NOT SPEAK ITS NAME

Saturday, September 21, 2002

I'm so nervous about this Tuesday dinner with Tony, scared that it will feel distant, or that he won't be able to deal. Did I quote Jason: *It's easy to be lovers, harder to be friends and much harder to be family?* And Tony doesn't want to work on any of the three. How can we build anything meaningful?

Thursday, September 26, 2002, 10:15 p.m.

Tony picked me up, we hugged and he said, *How are you doing?* I said, *I'm nervous.* He said, *Why,* and I let that sit. We talked in the car. At the restaurant he said, *So, what else is going on?* I said, *It'll come up.* Later, we relaxed and we were talking like friends. I wasn't sure if that was the right thing. The food made me nauseous, or maybe that was my nerves. I gave Tony the journal entries and said, *This is that project that's going to be published—it's kind of changed.* He said, *Maybe you should end it three weeks ago.* I asked him to call me right after he reads it to tell me what he's feeling.

Tony said, *How have you been the last few weeks—have you been better?* I said, *I don't know. I had this fantasy that the window into our new relationship would be that you would open up because you'd feel safer without the pressures and expectations of being boyfriends. Then I realized that the emotional intimacy was exactly what you didn't want, and I don't know where that leaves us.* He said he does want emotional intimacy, which sort of surprised me. Later, he said, *To a point.* I started to think that maybe we want the same result, except we disagree completely over the means. And he still wants control; I'm still basically operating on his terms. He made a good point about boyfriend relationships feeling artificial because you haven't really known the person that long and all the sudden he's so central to your life.

He said, *I want emotional intensity as long as it doesn't mean drama.* Then he said, *I've missed you,* which was sweet, really sweet and real and open. He said, *If in three or six months you feel like you're not getting enough out of our relationship, then we can reassess.* Then he asked if I was going to write another journal entry.

92

Trannyfags Unzipped
PATRICK CALIFIA

Once every two weeks, I get out a bottle of testosterone, a syringe and two needles. I clean the top of the bottle with rubbing alcohol and use the larger of the two needles to draw out my oily dose of the hormone. Then I switch to the smaller needle. My partner uses another alcohol pad to clean off the upper outer quadrant of my butt, and throws that needle deep into the muscle. The whole process takes less than ten minutes, but it took me four and a half decades to get here.

A year's worth of effects seen dramatic to me, but I don't always pass as male in public. Every time I shave, however, there's a little more hair on my face. Someday I'll be able to grow a beard like a proper bear. My shoulders are bigger, my butt is more narrow and flat and I have bigger muscles in my arms and legs. The savings account that will pay for chest surgery grows too slowly, but eventually I'll have $7,000 to make my shirts fit right.

The emotional and psychological changes created by testosterone are more subtle. Is my internal landscape shifting because I am finally doing something about my gender dysphoria, or is it T? My libido is outrageous. I have always supported decriminalization of prostitution and public sex, but now my understanding of these things is, shall we say, somewhat more visceral? I can jack off twice a day and still want a quick blowjob after lunch. My appreciation for hard-core porn and other eye candy has intensified. When somebody fuckable crosses my line of sight, they appear in sharp focus and bright colors, while everything else recedes into a dim background. I find it more difficult to cry. I don't have any problems with "'roid rage;" so far, my temper seems to have cooled quite a bit. But the potential for physical confrontation does not spook me as much as it used to.

Gay/bisexual female-to-male transsexuals (FTMs) are just starting to become more visible. This can be pretty jarring for gay men who base

THE LOVE THAT DARE NOT SPEAK ITS NAME

their common identity on having a dick. (While a few FTMs have genital surgery, most do not because it is so expensive, and the medical technology leaves a lot to be desired.) Transgendered queer men have enjoyed the most acceptance from groups that have questioned stereotypical body image or expanded their sexual expression beyond cocksucking and ass-fucking with a biophallus. I'm talking, of course, about bears, the leather or S/M community and fisters.

I feel blessed by the queer biomen are willing to explore sex with me. My good fortune is probably due to the fact that an experienced top is hard to find, and many of the trips I like to run (bondage, dirty talk, tit torture, shaving, flagellation, dildo play and handballing) are not dick-dependent. I tend to score better with guys who have done a lot of tricking. A genetic man with a rich history of man-to-man sex is less likely to be threatened by an encounter with somebody who was not born male. His queer identity is pretty unshakeable. By self-definition, whatever makes his dick get hard or his butthole twitch is homosexual.

Even when I have facial hair and a flat chest, there will be many xy gay men who will not want to accord me the courtesy of male pronouns. There's a lot of fear and loathing of female anatomy among Kinsey 6 fags. This kind of separatism hurts my feelings, but it is a little funny that the elegant architecture of the flesh between my legs has this much power to spook big bad daddies, even if I keep my 501s firmly buttoned. Even if I never get to suck cock at a sex club or sink into another willing furry butt, this gender transition would still be necessary. It is about my relationship to myself, which has to take priority over others' perceptions or opinions.

It's hard to explain what gender dysphoria feels like to somebody who has never experienced it. Most of us are too busy trying to fit into those "masculine" or "feminine," male/female categories to step back and ask why this system is so harsh and rigid. Gender dysphoria feels like something that was hard-wired, something I was born with. It appeared long before I heard about transsexuality, homosexuality or any sort of adult sexuality. I never understood why my parents kept referring to me as a girl, and I frequently told them that I was going be a man when I grew up. After being punished repeatedly for this, I learned to keep my mouth shut. I spent a lot of years trying to make myself feel bet-

94

ter by being a different kind of woman. But when I hit menopause and my doctor told me I should start taking estrogen, I couldn't do it. I could not deliberately put female hormones into my body. I had run out of options. I had to try T, had to see if making the male part of me more visible would ease the adversarial relationship I had with my biology.

Luckily, I live with someone who understands this struggle all too well. My lover and domestic partner is another FTM. He has been on hormones for several years and had chest surgery a while back. Matt has done a lot of public speaking about being a gay transman, and runs an Internet mailing list for trannyfags and their friends. He is determined to fulfill his own notion of what it means to be a man, and refuses to conform to other people's standards. We are raising a son who is Matt's biological child, conceived during a time in his life when he was not taking T.

We've encountered hostility about being parents, partly because our culture insists that children be indoctrinated into conventional gender expression and heterosexuality. Our son will probably grow up to be a butch straight guy, but he will know that he has choices. Some of Matt's friends, who had accepted him as male, had an especially hard time with validating that identity when he was pregnant. Matt's caustic reply to this was, "Oh, right, like you never told anyone you wanted to have his babies." Still, pregnancy was a pretty difficult experience for him, a major sacrifice he was willing to make because he wanted to be a parent so badly. Before I got involved with Matt, I assumed I would never raise a child, so this experience is a constant revelation to me, proof that life can always surprise me. The bond that I feel with our son is stronger than any other love I've experienced.

In some ways, my life is very domestic. I live with someone I love. I want to spend the rest of my life with him. We don't get out much because we are in baby world. But because we are transgendered men, we're a scandal. That is what the fight for sexual freedom is all about: The right to be left alone to enjoy the pleasures of an ordinary life.

FIFTEEN REASONS FOR REJECTING MY DICK
(AND MY RESPONSES)

THE LOVE THAT DARE NOT SPEAK ITS NAME

1. It's artificial.

This from somebody who can't get it up without a bottle of poppers and a tape in the VCR? Sure, you're Organic Boy himself.

2. It takes too long to put it on.

You go douche, I'll fool with the Velcro. We'll see who wins that race.

3. It's too hard.

'Cause a Viagra hard-on is so pliable and lifelike? Uh huh. Sorry, I'll go get that two-week-old zucchini out of the fridge. That oughta be floppy enough for ya.

4. It's too small.

Look in the drawer, stupid. I have things in there that will reach your prostate even if it's hiding in Hawaii.

5. It's too big.

Actually, no one has ever said this.

6. You won't be able to feel it.

No, it'll only give me goose bumps from my toes to my tonsils. If you can believe that your favorite porn star really did shoot for eight straight minutes in his latest video, honey, trust me. There won't be any credibility problem when I get off.

7. It isn't real.

Yeah, sex is all about what's "real." Because that guy on the cover of your bear magazine really is a truck driver, and all the men who pose in *Playgirl* are tops? And when you close your eyes, you are thinking only

96

ESSAYS ON QUEER DESIRE AND SEXUALITY

of the very special person you are with and what he is doing in the moment to pour all his love into your tender flesh.

8.   You can't cum inside of me.

OK, you win. Here's cab fare and my therapist's phone number. See you on the cover of *POZ*.

9.   Where's the romance?

It's extremely unlikely I would fall in love with anybody who couldn't take eight inches. Consider this your audition for True Love.

10. I have a latex allergy.

Can you say, "Avanti?" Or "silicone?" Or "fingers?"

11. What will the other boys think?

How are the other boys going to find out? I don't plan to take any ads out in the local gay rag.

12. It just doesn't turn me on.

Which is why your dick is pointing at your eyebrows, hmm? Precum never lies, Jack. You had to elbow six other people out of the way to talk to me. You knew perfectly well I was a tranny, and I bet you last bought somebody else a drink in 1986. We swapped so much spit on the way to my house that I could tell you your blood type. Whatever!

13. I'm afraid it will hurt.

Foreplay R Us. I own stock in Liquid Silk, Sex Grease and Probe. If you want it to hurt, you're going to have to ask very, very nicely, and make it worth my while.

97

THE LOVE THAT DARE NOT SPEAK ITS NAME

14.   Can we just fist fuck?

Will you marry me?
15.   I don't like to get fucked. I'd rather fuck you instead.

I'm a top, but I'm not stupid.

The Sluts of San Francisco

SIMON SHEPPARD

I'm in the ornate Castro Theater, at a matinee during the *San Francisco International Lesbian and Gay Film Festival.* My lover is sitting to my left, a cute stranger to my right. Cute Stranger and I chatted a bit before the film started, whilst my boyfriend was out popcorning. I'd even told the guy he was cute; he blushed when he said, "Thanks." Cute. Cute, cute, cute.

Partway through the film, I figure *what the hell* and let my hand trail, discreetly, down toward Cute Stranger's left leg. It makes contact mid-thigh. No reaction. I apply more pressure. He must notice, but his leg doesn't move.

My hand starts stroking, squeezing, moving crotchward; you know the drill. I get my hand between his thighs. He squeezes. I'm touching his denim-clad balls. I look over at my partner. We have a totally open, totally loving relationship, and he wouldn't mind what I'm up to. (Indeed, when I tell him the story later, he just smiles and asks for more details.) But I want this to be furtive, and I don't want Cute Stranger to get flustered. Especially now that I've discovered that his dick is hard as stone. Life is good.

My partner's had enough of movies; it's midway through the festival, we've both seen a lot of films, and he's not enjoying this particular program all that much. He whispers, "See you later, I'm going to the gym," and takes off. Because it's not all that popular a film, that leaves only Cute Stranger and me in the row.

Within a few minutes, I've slid my leather jacket across his lap, unbuttoned his 501s, and tugged down his briefs. His cock feels great—hefty, well-formed and hot. There's precum at the tip. For the next half-hour or so, I stroke and squeeze his cock. He sighs and moans softly, cuddles up, puts his arm around my shoulders, leans his head against mine. It's romantic.

THE LOVE THAT DARE NOT SPEAK ITS NAME

I'm doing my best to keep him on the brink without actually making him come, reading his dick's reactions like his crotch is in Braille. Can't create a mess.

The film, which is transgressively enough a documentary on gay youth, comes to a close. I take my hand away, leaving the jacket on Cute Stranger's lap, and he buttons up as the final credits roll. When the lights come up, he smiles and says, "That's the only way to see a movie."

"I hope we sit next to each other again sometime," I say.

"Maybe," he says, kisses me on the lips and makes for the exit. That's it. Anonymous, promiscuous sex, right there in public. And it makes me blissfully happy.

Queer sex was once, believe it or not, viewed as an act of political rebellion. In the early, palmy days of gay liberation, sex-radical manifestos celebrated the "revolutionary" potential of male-male sex. Sodomy versus patriarchy. Or as one slogan had it, "Up the ass of the ruling class."

Orgasm now! If consumer capitalism thrives on delayed gratification, orgy rooms do not. And back in the1970s, San Francisco was just one giant orgy room, or so nostalgia would have us believe. Homosex was everywhere, and it seemed only Armistead Maupin actually had a job.

Those were the days when I came of sexual age. I'd come out as a direct result of reading about Stonewall. I'd moved to San Francisco and lived in a queer commune. I was, I admit it, a child of the age. They were innocent times, when the aftermath of an evening of fellatio at the Boot Camp Bar or fisting at the Slot could be undone by a good night's rest and maybe a visit to the clap clinic. But within a short decade, the Edenic orgy came crashing down, straight into a swamp of viral death. Way back in1982, I was editor of the program book of what was then called the *San Francisco Lesbian/Gay Freedom Day Parade*, back before "pride" morphed from a deadly sin to a political agenda. On the very last page, there was a short article warning of a mysterious new disease that had begun cropping up among gay men. That was just before the deluge, before everything changed. Gay men, just emerging from a millennia of oppression, were still fighting the battle against shame when—Boom!—the wages of sin became plain to see on the faces of frail

ESSAYS ON QUEER DESIRE AND SEXUALITY

men stumbling through the Castro. The unspeakable had crashed the party.

We began marching around in ACT-UP T-shirts that read "Silence = Death," but in our heart of hearts there was the unspoken, ghastly knowledge that sex, too, could equal death. In the late 1980s, things got god-awful grim on the fuck front.

We queers had once done our time in high schools where the good girls/sluts dichotomy held sway. But we'd broken free to become happy, proud sluts ourselves. And now, our enemies cackled and we were paying the price.

Outdoor cruising spots got defoliated. The bathhouses got shut down. As leathermen died off, the stand-up-sex backroom bars South of Market disappeared, too. Tumbleweeds blew down the empty reaches of Castro Street.

Sluts, those of us who survived, went out of style.

The threat of HIV was (and is) real and deadly. But the epidemic also was seized upon as an instrument of control, both by assimilationists within the queer community who wanted us all to behave like good girls, and by those in the larger heterocentrist culture who were simultaneously envious of and repelled by men who numbered their sex partners in the dozens. Or hundreds. Or thousands.

Due in part to the response to AIDS, many more men came out, always a desirable thing. But a goodly share of them were less sex-positive than those who'd gone before, and some young queers bitterly blamed their enforced self-restraint on men they decried as old libertines. And it turned out that the ruling class, too, had its fair share of homos, and not all of them wanted to rock the yacht.

Many Respectable Gay Leaders proclaimed that we were really no different from everyone else, that our pre-HIV carousings were just growing pains. The erstwhile immature sowing of wild oats, they said, had been a symptom of the internalized homophobia that had robbed us of self-respect.

Sexual radicalism was supposedly defunct, derided as another dead-end of a failed countercultural moment. In place of the sixties' genderflex hippies in the Haight, the seventies' gay radicals and the eighties' self-consciously butch clones with poppers stuck up their noses, the

101

THE LOVE THAT DARE NOT SPEAK ITS NAME

new face of the queer movement was responsible folks making responsible demands. Gay marriage. Gay adoption. A place at the table. A place in the ranks. A broader, sadder-but-wiser queer community demanded every right that hets have, even the right to be boringly desexualized.

Gays began settling down in monogamously coupled bliss. Some moved to the 'burbs, bought that BMW, spent their days at IKEA and the MCC. Given the large proportion of het marriages that crash and burn, it should come as no surprise that many of these domestic arrangements didn't last as long as hoped. Some did, though, and more power to 'em. As long as it stems from true mutual desire, not just jealousy and fear, monogamy is a fine thing. Sometimes it even works out.

But not everyone longs to raise rug-rats and exchange vows in church. And sluts should have rights, too. When Rosie O'Donnell finally, finally, finally came out, she didn't do so for the sake of her queer brethren and sistren, nor as a challenge to straight hegemony. She came out for the sake of The Children, deriding as "gay Nazis" the more radical queers who'd urged to decloset for years. Thanks a whole fucking lot, hon.

A couple of years ago, my partner and I decided that 25 years was long enough to live in sin, so we got hitched at one of those City Hall group-commitment-ceremony extravaganzas. Despite our initial ambivalence, the ceremony was actually rather lovely. And then we headed down to the reception. The party room featured a photo display titled "Love Makes a Family," or something close. The photos all pictured pair-bonded same sex couples embracing at least one child.

Even then, even there, I felt marginalized. I did not see myself in those pictures. I did not see what would have passed as my partner's and my "family" at the time, which included me, William, his two long-term fuckbuddies, the young man I was tying up and spanking every week or three and an extended family of other tricks, nonsexual pals and sometimes-fuckbuds. The fix was in. We sluts were second-class queers. The good girls held sway. Sodomy had gone from being a threat to het power to a laugh-tracked joke on *Will and Grace*.

The public, civil-rightsy, fund-raising, PFLAGed face of queer America doth strive mightily to make us all sound respectable as can be. "AIDS

ESSAYS ON QUEER DESIRE AND SEXUALITY

has taught us a terrible lesson, and so we've decided to grow up and lead sex lives as unadventurous and inoffensive as, well, the rest of you." But you can only hold your breath for so long. A funny thing happened on the way to respectability: lots of gay men starting having sex again. Lots of sex.

A confluence of factors—some good, some not so good—have resuscitated queer sluttishness. First came battle fatigue and the dawning realization that the epidemic was going to be around for a long time to come, so *carpe diem*, dammit. Then came the rise of the Internet; in a place like San Francisco, getting laid via AOL is as easy as ordering a pizza. (Assuming that the pizza delivery boy stands you up half the time.) The rise of new drug regimes has made HIV seem less threatening, even though it's still plenty deadly. And despite all the rear-guard backlash against sodomy, the discourse around sexuality has broadened greatly over three decades. What was once unspeakable is now just more fodder for talk-shows. *Queer As Folk* is a hit. Sex, including gay sex and kinky sex, just won't shut up, though whether this is what Herbert Marcuse dubbed "repressive tolerance" is worth pondering.

And, as any female-to-male transsexual can tell you, testosterone gives guys the souls of sex pigs, no matter how polished the facade; even conservative homo Andrew Sullivan, who'd been hectoring us to grow up and settle down, got caught posting ads on a barebacking Website.

But most of all, the gay sluts are back because sexual pleasure—the giving and taking of erotic delight—is just plain (if not simply) good. That's not to say that all the club boys are tweaking toward Utopia. There are plenty of serpents in Eden redux: drug-resistant Gonorrhea, rampant speed addiction, sex that's not just promiscuous but harmfully compulsive. Most alarmingly, there's been a quantum increase in unprotected anal sex, not only between those already HIV-infected, but amongst the not-yets as well. The people I've spoken to who work in AIDS prevention programs do indeed confirm what we all already knew: queer men are having more sex, and less of it is condomized. One artist who's celebrated the gay sexual underground for the last quarter century says, "I thought we'd learned something, but apparently we have to go through it all again. It's like watching the replay of a train wreck, in slow motion."

103

THE LOVE THAT DARE NOT SPEAK ITS NAME

One argument for gay marriage is that officially ennobling (theoretically monogamous) male-male relationships would decrease "promiscuity" and thereby reduce HIV infections. The theory may well have a grain of truth, but it recruits the virus to enforce moralistic notions that "Good Girls Say No." Fuck that. "The consequences of non-monogamy are terrible," says Dr. Tom Coburn, one of George Dubbya's chief AIDS advisors. "It tears up relationships and can make people vulnerable to STDs." Well, sure, the STD thing is true: lifelong monogamy is a damn good way to guard against anal warts. But there's clearly a moralizing agenda at work here, too, the kind of antisex Pecksniffery that makes some of us want to go out and get gang-banged—with condoms—just for the hell of it. So how to keep queer men safer while not joining hands with the anti-sexers and homophobes? It can be a delicate balancing act; public health officials who sound even a little alarmist about the current state of affairs have been lambasted by more than a few queers.

Sure, the renaissance of unapologetic homolust is not without risks, but neither is it without rewards. All sorts of things are life-threatening—cigarettes, Big Macs, SUVs—but few are nearly as much fun as getting fucked. And yet, and yet . . .

One of my favorite fuckbuddies called me the other day. Turns out that another of his tops called him to say he'd been exposed to gonorrhea. It turns out that my pal, theoretically HIV negative, has been getting fucked by the guy without a rubber.

"So much for your celebration of gay sluts," he said.

"I never told you not to use a condom," I parried, and though I tastefully restrained myself, I felt like adding, "you idiot."

I feel fortunate in having enough self-control to maintain safe practices, in being able to integrate a fair amount of sex into a happy life, in being strong enough to shrug off some of the inevitable bumps and thumps along the path to perdition. It's not a matter of superior virtue, just the luck of the draw.

I'm getting older, and that's a hell of a thing to navigate out in the high seas of sex. Do the cruelties and rudenesses of tricking get to me sometimes? Well, of course they do, dear. But I guess I lack the energy to maintain a cynical facade. Maybe I'm a true romantic. Or maybe I'm just

ESSAYS ON QUEER DESIRE AND SEXUALITY

an old lecher with a heart of gold. Hey, is there a difference?

The gay sluts are back, and God bless us every one. We're a little bedraggled, maybe, but bravely marching toward the future, hard-ons in hand. Yes, I'm thoroughly happy to be in a wonderful, very-long-term relationship with a great guy. But I'm also totally thrilled that I've had sex with hundreds of men in my lifetime. (Maybe even more, but who's keeping count?) Now that I'm approaching—as the song says—"the autumn of my years," I'm grateful for all the dick my life has seen. Not every man was like that song's line about "vintage wine." Some were like a quick shot of espresso, some like too much beer, some like flat Coca-Cola. And some like perfectly chilled Tattinger. No problem. Men are like snowflakes; no two are alike. And each has something to offer. One of the great things about being a pariah is that you don't *have* to play by the rules. And one of the best things about being a queer man, even better than going to Palm Springs or idolizing Cher, is having sex with other men, be it one in a lifetime or three in one night. More than demonstrations and parades, trendy clothes and trendier DJs, gay bingo and bowling leagues, drag queens and leather queens, maybe even more than love and community, the one thing that gay men share is queer desire. All the varieties of queer desire. And fuck it, there's nothing wrong with that.

Cocksucking will most likely never regain its revolutionary cachet. My own sex life will, no doubt, grind to a stop somewhere along the inevitable shuffle to the grave. As will yours, gentle reader. But gay sexuality, once exiled to medical journals and would-be marriage beds, is back where it belongs—in queer hearts, minds, souls, bedrooms, backrooms, tearooms, sex clubs, dark parks, bright beaches, honeymoon suites, cheap hotels, bus stops, locker rooms and wherever else two men look at each other and think, "Oh, yummy." So tonight, my dear and wonderful, brave and foolish fellow sluts, let's all make love in San Francisco—or London, Kyoto, Quebec, New Delhi or Frostbite Falls.

And live to tell the tale.

In Difference

FRANCISCO IBÁÑEZ-CARRASCO

In May 2002, I had to be circumcised. Although the health reasons for this tardy excision are not of great consequence, the meaning of a nick in one's collar should not go unexamined, I think. It is about health and hygiene, about becoming older and having fucked a lot. A briss at forty means losing "an edge"—and losing it somewhat resignedly. We gay men pay a high cost to maintain the nimble architecture of our bodies, our pride and the virtual acceptance from others. We have followed the Greek regimen of food, sexual relations and treadmills that Michel Foucault described in *The Use of Pleasure*. Even those of us who are forced early to see the imminence of aging, illness and death, seek shelter in virtual greenhouses where we are served drug libations. On the flip side of this limpid screen, CNN flickers a phantasmagoria of ruined worlds, Africa decimated by HIV, wars in the Middle East, environmental disasters and intolerance everywhere.

Against this penurious global backdrop, what sense could we make of our/their acceptance of what being gay is? I think this acceptance, by others and ourselves, is in fact indifference, a postmodern surrogate value, a side effect of globalization. It marks what Naomi Klein calls "the triumph of identity marketing" (2000) and Denis Altman calls the "globalization of sexual identities" (2001). In Western(ized) societies, the slow departure from *camp* as a tool of militancy—ACT UP having been one of its last bastions—is one of the signals of the ending of queer as perverse outcast and the beginning of queer as commodity. Now, fully implicated in normalcy, we participate in the institutionalization and export of violence of the military and police forces, in the imposition of our views of safe sex and prevention on other cultures through AIDS philanthropy, and in wedlock modeled after the patently disastrous heterosexual contract. We are distinguished PTA parents, and we join the ladies who lunch—I'll drink to that! We say, we will not *dig* our graves in the macabre ground zero of the rectum; we will not let our ghosts dance a chilling techno anthem upon our grave. Normally, you can procreate at the nearest clinic (provided you have the dough). A new kind of "Leave it to Beaver" family, and like all families, a bit totalitarian, is being enforced through social bonding, progressive laws and artificial insemination. It's peculiar how a thought forged in the image of my Frankenstein prick can shift passively its aggressive position to an accepting missionary one of my rectum as a well of sanctity, useless for procreation or dissemination, but clean—finally, clean!

When I teach university students and tell them I am a gay man living with HIV since 1985, when I was twenty-two years old, and living with AIDS since 1993, they do not seem surprised—they aren't. They are indifferent. Students are not indifferent to what I teach; after all, they will need the grade (and some of them—poor fools—still seem to think they came to a university to engage in traditional pedagogy instead of an instructional deal). New generations are indifferent to *my desire*, and probably to theirs. Don't get me wrong, boys get their hard-ons, girls indulge as much as they did or didn't a few decades ago depending on their cultural heritage and social standing. What has changed is *the tone and intention of desire.* Young folks do not seem indifferent to homosexuality, or even sex; they seem indifferent to *desire*. What Craig Owens foreshadowed in 1983 has finally come to pass: "Pluralism, however, reduces us to being an other among others; it is not a recognition, but a reduction [of] difference to absolute indifference, equivalence, [and] interchangeability." Yes, sis and bros, if ya'll synchronize yer cultural production of desire ya'll be one and the same, some sort of Borg—if one is suffering, we all do; if one is pleased, we all are—but no one is, not really.

Indifference, the placebo effect of harm-reduction, our response for every tension, conflict and emergency, makes for a fine aphrodisiac—a nasty gateway drug. Sex and sexuality become a profoundly individualistic affair with no One. Isn't this what the homosexual agenda had planned: If you are white, or "of color" and middle class, educated and in an urban center, you have some legal reassurances that you will not be imprisoned or even verbally judged for spreading butterfly upon nests of barbed wire, whiplashes and honey. Freedom at last? After the

THE LOVE THAT DARE NOT SPEAK ITS NAME

tremendous queer bereavement and mobilization of the 1980s and 1990s in North America, we seem to think and practise sexuality as one autonomous entitlement to fuck and be fucked. I mean *any kind of fucking*, without any accountability to others or to ourselves. Is this indifference to desire some sort of whiplash effect? We seem willing to see the qualities of personhood—common sense, imagination, intuition, memory, reason, merit and compassion—travestied into indifference. Indifference: a surrogate for any of those qualities, and for freedom, empowerment and understanding. Indifference is indeed, tolerance and charity. A fantasy. An illusion of inclusion and a mirage of what John Ralston Saul calls "equilibrium." Oh—indeed—how deluded we must be.

Even the radicalism of *barebacking*—what some of us practised as militancy against the death, the oppressive laws of safe sex and the self-righteous normality of our generational peers—seems to have become not more than a *folie à deux* that is devoid of accomplice desire. Barebacking, the sweet budding of carnivorous flowers in our river banks, our phone lines and our Internet highway has been declared to be either misguided romance of the young and invincible, cultural resistance in the holes of gay men, or the eroticization of disease and death—what has been called "love as an affliction" and is often tagged with "seduction as infection." They say barebacking is caused by too much medical optimism, that it is a transgressive by-product of controlling safe(r) sex education; it has even been seen as one more compulsive social dynamic produced by accelerated technology. Didn't we come up with sex as contact/extreme sport; weren't we the avant-garde of speed-dating and fuck-buddying? Whatever it is, fucking skin on skin could be mistakenly placed in a cartography of free desire while it is firmly planted within the vast territory of the closet, which is presently a colonized space.

How can one fuck "safely" within the homosexual ghetto? How does this fucking of ghosts in a semi-transparent freedom, a penumbra, affect us all? Isn't freedom ultimately freedom, no matter how one looks at it? The closet, what used to be the precarious haven of the oppressed—Anne Frank's attic is now a public flop-house. Anyone can be/*will be* in the closet now. Discreetly, we feast on the exposed carnivo-

ESSAYS ON QUEER DESIRE AND SEXUALITY

rous flowers, a feast that dare not speak its name, unless the name is heterosexual, then, "barebacking" is simply called "sex." Whether an epi-
demiological trend or a macabre fashion, barebacking has been made
possible by having made other areas of our queer lives safe, livable, suburban, and commonplace—*Feng Shuied*, as it were. We have exiled the
poets and the satirists from the closet and now we are wondering, ageing and bored, through the deserts for forty days and forty nights seeing
the mirage of all that seems plentiful and free. We must be in need of
finding new ways *out of* this trite scene—new ways of being
obscene—because the closet does not exist any longer.

In the classroom, in the field (as a social science researcher) or as
AIDS activist, I am often treated with a muted degree of respect because
we are well-trained to respond to patriarchal signs. Once claimed, some
deference is afforded to my schooling, gray hair, civil manners and
cleanliness, and even to my "lived experience" as a "disabled" immigrant—being HIV at the right time at the right place—all the social
markers learned in what in 1996 Cindy Patton described as the "the pedagogy of a good citizen." My western repertoire of characters commands
a degree of legitimacy, authority, if nothing else, a degree of tolerance.
However, where am I to fit my superfluity of actions, motivations and
virus? My spontaneous combustion at the touch of a male skin, the
smorgasbord of the mixed South/North sexual culture in which I evolve,
or my ambivalent and queer values—where do they fit? Up my arse?

Indifference, the pseudo-quality, resides in the importance of being
earnest at listening and not hearing—silence. Active listening is an
annoying and anal-retentive Anglo habit in which we are often trained.
I have learned my lesson. I listen solicitously to variations of a comment
that I often get from people I encounter: "When I look at you, I think it
is good to have AIDS"—these comments often from apparently non-
queer, non-gay individuals. It's chilling to see the comfort that people
take in my living. In fact, my befuddled response is often something like,
"Oh, don't say that. It's about having a passion for living"—soap opera
standard fare. As the stomach turns, HIV has forced me to premeditate,
to be at times militant, at times a coward. It has made me a political and
sexual animal, interested in limits, drugs, body calisthenics, privacy and
sleaze. Infection, the great contraceptive to indifference, makes me test

109

THE LOVE THAT DARE NOT SPEAK ITS NAME

the necessary limits to freedom. It has been hard work that I would have probably never done, if I didn't have to. Indifference is a weak option; it is not a value. It is the anti-value. If I had listened attentively to the silence of the men I have fucked, I would have infected many more men than I probably have—getting potential tricks to talk is difficult.

Indifference is the postmodern gossip; it spreads viciously. In June of 2002, I was interviewed for a entry level teaching position at York University. Aside from the usual absurdness of pretending that a group of socially inept academics can assess one's merit in a few hours, this interview staged an intriguing role reversal. I sketched my views on health education, both at the academic and school level by making connections with my experience as educator and researcher. I talked about HIV and STDs and prevention in the context of youth and education. A woman in the search committee began to repeatedly formulate an accusation in the guise of a question: "You point at the negative effects of health education," she asked. "What about the good aspects?" She assured our audience that "we are all here because of sex" and pointing an stern finger at me she added, "You say 'joy and seduction' are 'a good thing' and you don't give any evidence of how you might cover this in your teaching of health education." Insidious move, that was. Suddenly, I, the self-confessed whore, who conceptualizes desire as I penetrate, straddle, thrust and disseminate each deliverable milliliter of my infected and indulgent being, was turned into some sort of sex hating ogre.

Although I am used to the consensual idea/activity of bonding and beating, I couldn't react quickly to this attack, strapped as I was in my potential employee position. Later, I realized that opening up the closet for all bleeding-hearts to use "queer theory" has enabled conservative individuals to perform curious somersaults—Gimme back to the lions and the Christians! When the agitated examiner—mentally christened "Miss Joy and Seduction"—said that sex "is good thing," she said it as *literally* as Martha Stewart does. When she said that we all come from sex, she meant that sex is "reproductive." Thus, when I say that I would educate children, youth and adults in the idea of *anxiety* and *uncertainty* of health, dis-ease, living and dying, and particularly the joys and *perils* and of sexuality. I am literally taken for a ride. I cannot even begin to make a difference here between "instructing" about sex, sexuality and sexual health, and a pedagogy of desire—Miss Joy and Seduction, by the way, is not an expert on Health Education. In my York University interview, I was too negative to fit in a Sesame Street world of nice pedagogy. Weeks later, I found out through the grapevine that this woman might be a closeted lesbian. Literal-mindedness is one symptom of queers losing an edge; we must be good and normal people—literally. One of the conditions of normalcy is that sex is always rosy and good. The closet is becoming a *Disneyfied* territory; we must be in need of new breeding grounds. Incidentally, I did not get the job. Bitter? Yes! And all the wiser.

In "The Double Flame" (1993) Octavio Paz, the Mexican Nobel laureate tells that "Death is inseparable from pleasure, and Thanatos is the shadow of Eros. Sexuality is the response to death: cells unite to form another cell and hereby perpetuate themselves." We should go out and get laid more often. There should be more sexuality and sex, and it should be more obscene. We are exposed permanently to the neon gore of violence and pain—think video games, talk shows and the six o'clock news—why wouldn't we crave it? Should we live sex and sexuality vicariously? Will we know what to do when we are confronted with fatal attractions? There is such a thing as too much life. It is like the eruption of the engorged entrails of a volcano, particularly in our teens and twenties. Yes, there is such a thing as too much life that makes us invincible, if only momentarily, and wild in its plenitude. At turbulent times, we might not see clearly or understand precisely, but there is no rule that dictates that we must be *one and whole* at one single point in our lives. Incompleteness, uncertainty and anxiety prevail—they often are at the root of faith. At the peak of youth, we should be indifferent neither to Eros nor to Thanatos.

As a teacher, I have been trained—and I have resisted at every blow—to engage students in sweet pedagogical strategies of mutual recognition and rapprochement between generations, in information and prevention. My colleagues and students often speak like Ms. Universe candidates who are running on a platform of goodness for all, equality, good food and protease inhibitors for African children and families, and wearing sensible shoes. Is there any other way of understanding poverty, mediocrity, pain, illness, drugs, joy, seduction, orgasms and other experiences than going through them? Sounds like I

THE LOVE THAT DARE NOT SPEAK ITS NAME

am saying, dear reader—Go! Trip the light fantastic. Get fucked and infected to see one truth. This is not very different from what North American teachers mean when they say "multiculturalism." Shake a black hand, have a conversation and your racism will dissipate. Well, I have given black, Indian, Asian and Latinos a hand—literally and metaphorically, get it?—and our shared racism and homophobia remain intact. Is our next step to have heterosexuals patting us on the back for being witty, preppy, cutesy and normal? We should remember to look at ourselves, our community of ghosts, and see how abnormal and different we are. I am referring to abnormality as a positive attribute, not as a sense of disgust, but as people who do not follow the convention, say heteronormativity. Our relations are valuable and strong but they are still outside the framework of social conventions—they should stay there.

Our indifference is more than just the soporific alchemy of two languages, one language of contraband of sex and desire that deals in words like "top" and "bottom," "closeted" or "out," "negative or "positive," and a modernist language that talk about integration, normality and suburban conventionality. Our indifference is the passive acceptance of assimilation. I see our values reside more in the "accentuated" queer experience that includes "codes of silence" and "recognitions" as explained by Hemming Bech in "When Men Meet." I see that the "boys club" in workplaces, ivory towers and social spaces remains as strong as ever, even in the apparent presence of tolerance and comfort with gay men. We have worked our asses off (and getting them infected along the way) to fill our roles in the narrow repertoire that has been offered to us: polite citizens, demons, victims, heroes or celebrities.

Naturally, most of us are not able to wear such designer's straight-jackets. My first lover was an unabashedly presumptuous, self-righteous and arrogant closeted Anglo gay man. He was a professor in the Faculty of Education at Simon Fraser University where I ended up as a graduate student for nearly ten cheerless years. Roger was HIV+ since the early 1980s, and about five years into his early retirement he came back to teaching because he needed to make money, I assume, to support two offspring from a second marriage, a drinking habit and a trail of young lovers who came before and after me. He died an alcoholic, his HIV hav-

ESSAYS ON QUEER DESIRE AND SEXUALITY

ing remained latent. The silence around his death was deafening. His colleagues ignored him—as they had always studiously ignored our cohabitation ten years earlier—and circled the wagons of indifference. A few polite notes were written and little or no memory of this man remains in that Faculty where I finished my doctorate. What's to be learned here? Whether they are baby boomers, generation Xers, or "rave twinkies," queers still tend to live strange and torturous lives. "Queer" becomes "normal" in our longing to fit the stereotypes made available to us. Homophobia, or mendacity by any other name, is well and alive. Having become indifferent to the strangeness of our ways, to the ways of fucking and caring for each other, we have timidly crossed over to the normal market culture. What used to be our ways of getting it on, court-ing, healing, infecting, assisting in our euthanasia or providing rites of passage, are being systematically squirted with a bubbly soft core.

Gay men fuck good. How come we are using one of our central cul-tural characteristics—promiscuity—only to sell advertisement for gor-geous POZ men, for anorexic androgynous boys, for packaged good taste? We fight against rules and regulations that are said to inhibit our precious individualism, our rights to fuck in public and private. We fight anyone who lets the wrong remark or joke escape their tight lips—like the eunuch piano player in a bawdy house, we police the language and the manners of others. We are slowly being allowed in schools with "Steve has two daddies" and "Jennifer has two mommies," a boring placebo to Britney Spears' ferocious tits-n-ass, to Eminem's pasty angry inch, to unabashed black misogyny in rap, to the male-geisha stereotype of Asians. We remain polite in our pedagogical mediocrity that white-washes our rich and complex sexual culture. There are signs of anes-thetic cultural mediocrity everywhere; we are shopping from an International Male catalogue and not laughing at the joke.

How can one compete with the phantasmagoria of car crashes, thug beatings, relentless thrusting of Lolitas, the pervasive immediate, and updating technology that fills us with banal information and indiscreet intimacy—too much information. You got that right, girl! I cannot com-pete. My partner, a noble Anglo-seronegative-working-class-gay-man, and I got together five years ago. We agreed that respect, not "Hello-Kitty love," the ridiculous packaged stuff they sell us at Valentine's day,

113

THE LOVE THAT DARE NOT SPEAK ITS NAME

was to be our bond; otherwise we would be insanely jealous because we could not compete with each other and there is always someone larger, limber, wittier, faster and richer. We could not satisfy each other's every social and sexual need. It might be the case that Octavio Paz is right and "[L]ove is a bet, a wild one, placed on freedom. Not my own; the freedom of the Other" and within this thought I make sense of the strategic uses of fucking as a weapon, drug, or mechanical device. However, I have a hard time accepting that some perfectly good fucking, erotic and nasty, might be squandered as a "natural" afterthought or a bodily function—one can often see gay nymphettes grow like Moonflowers at night, their crystal and languid limbs draped to collect the POZ morning dew. It is beautiful and natural, but queer sex—Alas! Sex in general, is far from natural (no matter what Miss Joy and Seduction says). There is a difference between our beloved promiscuity—perverse and compassionate Eros and love overflowing—and the silent and numbing desperation, forgetting and oblivion that abounds today. What makes the world we inhabit thrilling is the degree by which one is reminded that each one of us, in our relationship with others (and deeper into what Peter McLaren calls *enfleshment*), is different and yet not unique. Even in the arms of a chemist Morpheus, suspended from a jungle of leathers or catheter tubes—you choose your torture/pleasure of the flesh—one should not be indifferent to the incessant rustling of desire under the cloth. To be galvanized, sexuality must be premeditated and ambitious and compassionate and loving.

All I am left to show you, my kind reader, is how I take apart the everyday artifacts, like a hermit playing with the archeological remnants of a long gone empire, and how I reassemble them into some familiar, interconnected yet astonishingly novel thing. All I have to show is how lucidity, intentionality, intuition and imagination power these artifacts. It is hard to compete with indifference because it originates and is implemented with a million recognizable fragments of who we are. It sounds like we do, it walks like we do, and in the end, it leaves us with an impostor. Those artifacts have allowed me to survive AIDS, to not die young and exquisitely tragic (and in decadent credit card debt), to withstand not only the flight of the squeamish, the homophobics, but also the compassion turned into envy of the ones who never forgave me to have

114

survived and moved on.

Two days after I started writing the first draft for this piece I slowly unveiled my born-again masculinity to the world: gory, seething, tender and bruised, ready to commit mischief and penitence. My partner, John, said that it had turned its fashion, from turtle neck to crew cut, its *camp* was not lost on us. It is a cultural change, a brutal one, and like any other cultural change, like migration, like disappearance of innocence, like rape and wedlock, harvest and sowing, this change is full of uncertainty and potential. I have gained another weapon for the infected. I stand dazzled in the sight of the beauty of our weapons. It is dangerous to put an exposed gun barrel in the hands of a man in love with other men. It is like winding up, once again, his arrested adolescence. It's been a decade-long *Dog Day Afternoon* and I have dogged my way through it—you know what I mean. I have robbed to save deranged homosexuals who surgically want to become queens. I do not look at this world with indifference because it is not the way the world and its inhabitants should look at me, no matter how much they reassure me of my normality.

My Life as a Girl
MICHAEL ROWE

Last January, I came upon the photographs of myself as very young girl in a box in my father's study when I was visiting him in Victoria, British Columbia. They were tucked away in a yellow Kodak envelope, covered with a thick coating of dust and marked "Cuba, 1968."

My father had been accredited to the Canadian Embassy there in 1968; his second diplomatic posting in what would eventually become a long and illustrious career. Seeing the word "Cuba" written in long-faded black ink in my late mother's elegant scrawl momentarily halted my breath.

Gingerly, I withdrew the photographs from the envelope and stared at my six-year-old self.

In one photo, I am standing on the back of a tricycle being driven with macho determination by my younger brother, Eric. I am wearing a fur-trimmed hat and am carrying a basket.

In another, I am wearing a cowboy hat over a towel that streams down my back like long hair. I am drinking a glass of milk and looking up at the camera like a natural seductress.

In the third photo, I am standing in our driveway in the bright tropical sunlight wearing an old housedress over my khaki shorts and striped Buster Brown T-shirt. My hair is cut short, like a pixie's. My features are delicate and slender, and I am clutching a plush stuffed dog to my breast as though it were a baby. The expression on my face in this one is so ineffably tender, so sweet, so vulnerable and so *natural*, that my first impulse was to sweep the child in the photograph into my arms and run off with him

Him, not *her*. I am not now, nor have I ever been female. But I look down at the sweet face in the photograph, and I remember, and I feel like weeping.

ESSAYS ON QUEER DESIRE AND SEXUALITY

Before I ever heard the expression "gender dysphoria," or the word "transgender," I knew that I have been two people in my life, one male, one female.

I've always loved the Native-American expression "two-spirited," which has of late been appropriated by many gay social historians in an earnest drive to document the acceptance of homosexuality by ancient cultures. The problem with this approach is the application of twentieth century gay cultural definition, which in this instance, seeks to claim "two-spiritedness" as a defacto manifestation of homosexuality as it is currently defined.

The term "two-spirited" has suggested the presence of both male and female "spirits" in the body of one man or one woman. This lies in direct contradiction to the contemporary gay masculinist assertion that homosexuality is its own sexual orientation—uniquely male—and exists without reference to the opposite gender.

The emotional component to this argument is rooted in justifiable rage and frustration at years of gay men being told that their orientation made them "less than men," more "womanly" and therefore inferior. For gay men who subscribe to this masculinist ideal, there is little room for allowance of the notion that there might be a female presence in the equation. In fact, the disdain that many gay men manifest towards effeminacy often rivals that of their straight peers. In the "testosterone revolution" of the 1970's, when gay men *en masse* flocked to gyms, cut their hair short, grew moustaches and dressed to out-butch their own sissy history—in jeans and lumberjack shirts and leather—a new physical ideal was born and there was little quarter accorded to those gay men who wouldn't (or couldn't) live up to it. In retrospect, there was an edge of hysteria to it that wasn't often discussed in those days.

It is with some relief that I note that today's gay youth, in their enthusiasm for the reclamation of "queer space" have largely abandoned these strict notions of masculinity and femininity, and many of them look at the ageing remnants of this "Village People" clone era with the same amused frustration that teenagers show to their hopelessly out-of-date parents. Big muscles and being "straight-looking and acting" don't carry the cachet they once did, as twenty-something gay men redefine not only the very notion of what queerness can mean, but also

117

THE LOVE THAT DARE NOT SPEAK ITS NAME

notions of beauty, masculinity and desirability.

When I was a little boy, I looked out at the world through a girl's eyes. It might have been my secret if I thought there was anything special about it, but I never did. There was a little girl in my head, and she lived in a secret place behind my eyes. She was as natural and real as anything in my world, and I liked who she was—who *I* was.

I had access to dolls because my parents were modern, evolved people who felt that they were encouraging my nurturing instincts which would, in the fullness of time, make me a good father. I had access to my mother's dresses and jewelry because she thought I was creative and theatrical. The place behind my eyes where I took these things to play was neither theatrical nor bent on any future thoughts of being a father. It was an effortlessly feminine place where I was just myself.

My gender was as natural and uncomplicated to me as it would have been to any other girl, except in the memorable moments when my parents would exasperatedly point our that I was "a *B-O-Y*, not a *G-I-R-L!*" and they would always spell it out for me, for emphasis.

I would retort that I didn't want to be a boy, and I wouldn't be one. At that age, in my mind, it was still a choice.

I received my first Barbie at Christmas in 1968, after much swooning over the *Sears Christmas Wish Book*. I wanted a Barbie with long, ash-blonde hair, and there was a beautiful one who came dressed in a red fishnet one-piece and a beach bag. I didn't, however, bat an eyelash when Sears ran out of stock on that particular model and substituted a Twiggy doll instead, with short, blonde hair and a mod green-and-blue mini-dress, looking remarkably like the eponymous 60's supermodel upon whom it was based. I thought she was beautiful, and fear that I would still think so today. The moment was pure magic. The closest I ever came to fratricide was the morning I discovered that, in a fit of malicious pique, my brother had scribbled all over Twiggy's face with a blue ballpoint. My parents were furious with my brother, but there was no particular haste on their part to replace the doll.

One evening when I was about seven, I announced to my father that what I wanted to be when I grew up was a "lady teacher." Like many children I had developed an all-encompassing aesthetic crush on my

ESSAYS ON QUEER DESIRE AND SEXUALITY

teacher, who was dark-haired and pretty, and who corrected my homework in pink pencil. Even when she wrote admonitions like *Pay attention!* in the margins, it seemed like a benediction because of the glorious rose-pink of that soft pencil.

My father is a jovial man, and a deft wordplayer. His rejoinder (which I know he thought was quite witty) was, "Well, Michael, I think that's a wonderful idea. You can be a 'lady teacher' all right."

I was euphoric at this endorsement of my career plans, and beamed up at him.

My father paused for a couple of beats then added with a flourish, "You can be a lady teacher, and *teach ladies!*"

He broke into explosive laughter at his own joke, oblivious to my devastation as I hit the first major wall of my childhood. My father is not, nor ever has been, a cruel man, and there is no way he could have known the effect his joke had on me. My life at that age was a smooth, unbroken surface, and there was no turmoil surging beneath for him to see. The internal storm that would erupt years later, threatening to split my sexual psyche in half, was still far out to sea, and nowhere in evidence at that point. The serenity of a child's logic can be its own balm. When you *know* you're a girl, and your worldview is completely female, you have no reason to question it until someone whose authority is unquestioned calls it into question.

I felt cold dread spread upwards from my belly as I realized that not only was my desire to grow up to be a "lady teacher" incorrect, it was so incorrect that the only response to it was explosive humor at the absurdity. An abyss yawned beneath me. My father's causal obviation of my dream was doubly threatening. Not only was my femininity dismissed; nothing was offered up in its place. I wouldn't ever be a *B-O-Y*. That wasn't an option in my mind. I thought of the boys and men I knew, all angles, jutting elbows and skinned knees, loud voices and war games, and shuddered. There was nothing there that I could relate to. No, what I was facing was the annihilation of my entire gender identity. In my mind, I was a girl, or I was nothing. And with that came the first stirrings of what would become a lifelong sense of guilt about not being able to be what everyone else seemed to demand.

As an embassy family, we were accorded two live-in servants, a

THE LOVE THAT DARE NOT SPEAK ITS NAME

maid-of-all-work named Berta, and a cook named Maria. The two women loved me in that way that older *latina* women often love very effeminate young boys. To my mother's bemusement they found me adorable, and to her chagrin they spoiled me beyond redemption. Berta and Maria worked hard all day for us, and although we considered them "members of the family," it seems doubtful in retrospect that *they* saw *us* that way. Children know when they're loved, however, and I had no doubt that they loved me. Best of all, they seemed to delight in my girl-ishness—my propensity for wearing my mother's clothes and shoes, my fondness for dolls, for playing school with me as the "lady teacher" and my plush animals and my benighted baby brother as my "class."

On weekends, Berta and Maria would undergo a miraculous meta-morphosis: they would transform themselves into *women with boyfriends*. Once they were dressed, they would invite me to their room to witness the finishing touches. The scent of their cheap face powder and lipstick, the flowery sweetness of their heavy perfume, the gardenias they tucked into their hairdos, signaled to me a world of transformative possibilities, as did the exaggerated, cheeky feminine sway of their hips as they high-heeled out of our home into the fragrant Havana night. My mother was beautiful, and I loved to watch her get dressed for an evening out with my father, but her restrained Yankee elegance was nothing compared to the overblown, meaty femaleness of the two women. Few modern authors have more beautifully rendered this breed of *latina* than the Chilean-Canadian writer Francisco Ibáñez-Carrasco in his luminous novel *Flesh Wounds and Purple Flowers*, where he describes "women who do the cha-cha down the sinuous sidewalk."

I approached Berta and Maria one afternoon with my gender dilem-ma. I wanted to be a girl, and everyone was telling me that I couldn't be one because I was a boy. How was I going to fix this?

They smiled and giggled, and told me they had an idea. There was a sawmill not far from the house. They could take me there, and the sawmill workers could cut off my penis with the whirling buzz saw. It might hurt a little, they said, but the solution was definitive.

I thought it was a marvelous idea, and joyously began to plan for my trip to the mill.

When Berta and Maria realized that their indulgent joke had gone a

ESSAYS ON QUEER DESIRE AND SEXUALITY

little too far they shushed me, frantically looking over the top of my head into the house to see if my mother had heard them, or heard me screaming with joy as I danced around the patio. They swore me to secrecy. As panic-stricken as they were at the thought of their inevitable dismissal, they were likely equally horrified by my enthusiasm for the "operation" they suggested. To me, it was a matter of no consequence. My penis was simply an obstacle to the world seeing me as I saw myself.

Once again, though, I felt the sting of disappointment as yet another adult held out a carrot, then snatched it away, laughing, and telling me not to be so silly.

Late one afternoon, shortly before we returned to Ottawa in the summer of 1969, my father took a series of photographs of my brother and me on our terrace by the pool to send to my grandparents in the United States.

My father must have been in a good mood, because when I put on my favorite housedress over my clothes and reached for Randy, my blue plush dog, and cuddled him, he didn't tell me to take of my dress because I was a *B-O-Y*, not a *G-I-R-L*. Instead, he kept shooting. In some of the photographs I am laughing, which suggests that we were having fun, and I was happy.

In my mind's eye, Randy was my baby, and I was his mother—and I was beautiful.

The red-gold sunlight sparkled on the blue surface of the swimming pool and played across my face, making my eyes very bright. Standing there in my dress, I lowered my head and smiled shyly, tilted my eyes upwards, and held the plush dog very close. In a way, I was as complete and organic in that transient moment as I have ever been since.

A shift began to occur internally when we returned from the cloistered world of diplomatic Havana and I began a suburban North American childhood. By eight, I had gradually become aware that I wasn't a girl, at least biologically, though what I actually was could be anyone's guess. I had begun to think in terms of a third sex (though that terminology would naturally not have been available to me). I never found my body incongruous, as many transgendered people do, and the trip to the sawmill had been long-since dismissed by me as an unnecessary sacri-

121

fice. I had no knowledge of female anatomy, and had a vague notion that naked girls were like baby dolls: smooth down below, with a small hole in their bottoms to pee out of. I was perfectly happy with my own willowy, boyish frame, and to me, the difference between me and the other boys was internal, though no less definitive for its invisibility. I was simply a different type of girl, and it didn't bother me in the slightest.

I wrote fan letters to David Cassidy, confidently suggesting that he be my boyfriend, even though I was a boy, urging him not to let that come between us and swearing I wouldn't either. I wore the shortest shorts I could, and when I stood in direct sunlight I pressed my legs together and made a skirt out of the shadow. I dreamed that I had glorious, long, auburn hair like a Beautiful Chrissy doll, or like Brenda Starr, Girl Reporter, whom I planned to become when I grew up. ("A crack reporter in high-fashion clothes!")

My identification with, and jealousy of, "other" little girls and "real" little girls was searing, even annihilating. I played with them at their games when they would have me, learning to skip with a pink rubber skipping rope, playing house and always refusing to be "the father" or "the husband" (I often played "the beautiful older sister," because I was larger than my female playmates), which the girls accepted with surprising equanimity, at least until just before puberty. I was green with envy when they came to school with ponytails tied up in brightly colored wool rope, or when their fathers called them "princess," or the boys treated them as delicate, and different. I was delicate and different, too, and I wanted to be treated that way.

My childhood after Cuba had become an odd admixture of impressions and contradictions. On one hand, my parents continued to indulge me, out of love, with dolls and tea sets. When I visited my grandparents in western New York, my *hausfrau* German grandmother allowed, even encouraged, me to wash the dishes and cook with her, and I became her little confidante. She even bought me my own apron, with a red heart embroidered on the pocket. My grandfather, the World War I veteran, on the other hand, kept his distance and eyed me warily, sensing quite rightly that something queer was afoot in his well-ordered house.

Closer to home, things got progressively tenser. My mother's fury one night at the fact that I'd left my Barbies out on the rec-room floor was

ESSAYS ON QUEER DESIRE AND SEXUALITY

awe-inspiring. As she shouted about the dolls, and how she had wanted a *son*, not a *daughter*, she grew apoplectic with rage. Her face grew red, and the tendons in her neck stood out like flushed marble columns. Her anger seemed to me out of sync with the crime at hand—the mess of dolls and doll clothes on the floor—which was relatively minor. It appeared to encompass the Barbies themselves and what they represented: aberrant toys for a boy, and the entire albatross of an indulged childhood she might understandably regret as she surveyed her young son, about whom nothing seemed normal. In fairness to my parents, "normalcy" didn't carry much currency in our family. I had already demonstrated a stunning precocity with writing and art, and I read voraciously, so there was a mental folder open where my parents could place my eccentricities. Even so, my mother was clearly growing tired of my weirdness. That Christmas, I received one more doll. My mother explained to me that this was a gift from my parents, not from Santa, because Santa didn't bring dolls to boys of my age. This was the last one, she assured me, ever.

I named the doll Clara, and cherished her until I turned 10, when I outgrew dolls altogether.

Betrayal of your gender is a fearsome crime, especially if you are a boy, and it is punishable by any number of cruel reparations. No one is in a better position to enforce these chastisements than unsupervised children in the harsh arena of the playground, and you never forget the first time it happens. Although there is a reluctant space in the social hierarchy of school life accorded to the tomboy, the word "tomgirl" is non-existent. In its place, there are words like *sissy, faggot, girl* and *gaylord.* When society teaches young boys that they are the elect sex, and that girls are pretty, decorative, desirable trophies to be hunted and speared, males who betray that divine right face the wrath of their tribe. It may be natural to *fuck* a girl, but God help you if you act like one, or wish you *were* one. As Quentin Crisp archly observed in *The Celluloid Closet,* Rob Epstein and Jeffrey Friedman's 1995 documentary on gays in Hollywood, "there's no crime like being a woman."

Young women, in their strawberry-scented quest to fulfill their part of the social bargain with the boys, are as merciless, perhaps even more

123

THE LOVE THAT DARE NOT SPEAK ITS NAME

pitiless, than their hunters. The high, cruel laughter of adolescent girls in the playground, the whiplash of their pretty, long hair, was tattooed into the flesh of my memory without the benefit of anesthetic.

In 1973, I was eleven. We had moved to Geneva, Switzerland where my father joined the Canadian Mission to the United Nations. I had been enrolled in the French *Lycee* section of College du Léman, an elite international Swiss private school catering largely to children of the diplomatic corps and the multinational business community, in addition to cast-off Hollywood kids whose parents were far too busy to raise them, and the scions of wealthy Iranians, including, it was rumored, minor royalty. The Iranian boys were usually lean and muscular, adept at soccer and precociously sexual and seductive. The Iranian girls wore make-up and high-fashion as a birthright, and with more natural panache than American women twice their age. The American girls were in the early-1970s in Maybelline mode: clean, straight hair parted in the center, Noxema complexions, with misty blue eye shadow and Bonne Bell Lip Smackers always at the ready. I thought they were all marvelous looking. The American boys were broad-shouldered jocks, classic "boyfriend" types in Adidas windbreakers and Levis. A lifelong love of American men, and a companion fetish for them, was likely born at some point in the autumn of 1973.

I arrived at school the first day wearing banana-yellow bell-bottoms, a white short-sleeve turtleneck and black platform shoes. I had taken to wearing a black, Kodak camera bag slung over my shoulder like a purse in homage to the leggy American girls I'd met that summer. My hair was cut straight across, in bangs, like a china doll. This variation on the bowl-cut was common in the early seventies, but with my delicate features, I must have looked precious. What causes me to marvel, from the vantage point of thirty years, is that I somehow thought I would be invisible, and that I looked as incongruous as anyone else.

As I alighted from my mother's car, a girl looked at me, pointed and nudged her friend. They laughed behind their fingers for a moment, then the first girl asked me if I was the new ambassador's son. Thinking that they were being friendly, I smiled and I told her that, no, I wasn't. Only later did I discover that the new ambassador's son was developmentally challenged, and that there was nothing benign in her question.

ESSAYS ON QUEER DESIRE AND SEXUALITY

My morning classes that first day were innocuous enough, and when the lunch bell rang, I went out to the schoolyard to eat the lunch my mother had packed. As I sat on a bench in the playground, a group of boys approached. They loomed over me, silhouetted in the sunlight. I squinted up at them, shielding my eyes with my hand.

"Are you a boy or a girl?" the leader asked. He had a rough voice, a definitively male voice, even at eleven. I'd learned that his name was Pedro, and he liked to fight.

"I'm a boy," I said indignantly. By then, I had learned the currency of language necessary to survive, and to enjoy the privacy of my inner world of unselfconscious femininity. Although I was frequently mistaken for a girl, it was important to assert that I wasn't one.

"You look like a fuckin' girl to me," he rasped. His friends broke out in ugly laughter behind him, and shuffled their feet.

Intuitively I smelled the implied offer of violence, and I felt the first answering tendrils of dread stir inside me. I stood up, prepared to conciliate, and was slapped across the mouth.

I recoiled, shocked by the pain, and tasted blood in my mouth. I touched my bruised lip and burst into tears, which I learned later in my career as an object of ridicule, is almost always a mistake.

"Awwwwww," Pedro whined. "Is the little girl gonna cry? Is she gonna go and *tell a teacher*? Huh? *Is* she?" There were raft of catcalls from his friends as I sobbed. I gathered my Kodak camera case up and slung it over my shoulder where it belonged. I faced him, and through my tears said the first thing that came to my mind.

"If you think I'm a *girl*," I sobbed, *"then you shouldn't have hit me. You don't hit girls."*

It might not have been the most useful answer, but it stunned the bullies with its perverse logic, and they left me alone after that, at least that particular group did.

Two things happened when I turned twelve, and both marked the end of my childhood, the beginning of my adolescence and the next stage of my gender evolution in a way that was profound and irrevocable.

The first was meeting Nancy, the girl who would become my defacto "big sister." She was the daughter of an American business executive,

125

THE LOVE THAT DARE NOT SPEAK ITS NAME

and my mother had met her mother at a meeting of the American Women's Club of Geneva. My mother had recently fired the live-in *au pair*, when the girl became pregnant by the Sardinian waiter she was dating on weekends This was likely less of a trauma for the *au pair* than it was for my mother — the fact that we lived in a villa on a hill in a small town outside of the city had clearly been an ordeal for the young woman, and she was likely well rid of us. I know she suspected that I rummaged through her makeup drawer when she wasn't around, exploring the process by which she became so pretty every morning and alluring beyond mere words when she went out on weekends — and she wasn't wrong.

My parents entertained a great deal, and were often out at embassy parties and diplomatic receptions themselves. With no one to watch my brother and me on those evenings, my mother was disadvantaged. She solved this problem by hiring a series of young American girls, the teenage daughters of her friends, to baby-sit us. They were all very pleasant, but when my favorite graduated from our school and went home to the States for college, I was bereft. And then my mother hired Nancy and my life changed.

From our first meeting, Nancy *got* me. She *understood* me, and whatever she might not have understood, she accepted swiftly and silently. She thought I was adorable, and I thought the sun rose and set on her. A night when Nancy came to baby-sit was better than Christmas, and if she stayed for the weekend, it was beyond anything as pedestrian as bliss. I idolized her. Our talks were all-encompassing, and anything she could do, I wanted to learn. She taught me how to knit, how to appreciate tea, how to love music. When she failed to teach me how to play the guitar, she wrote a song for me instead. When she failed to help me understand mathematics, she said it was OK. She gave me gothic novels and saucy stewardess books like *Coffee, Tea, or Me* and *The Fly Girls.* She introduced me to a new writer named Stephen King one evening when she brought over a sophisticated novel that had just been published about a young high school outcast who discovered telekinetic powers when she began to menstruate. I immediately identified with the protagonist, and felt terribly grown up when Nancy lent it to me after she was done. I managed to read it from cover to cover before my mother

ESSAYS ON QUEER DESIRE AND SEXUALITY

picked it up and declared it "too racy" a book for me.

Nancy taught me how to write poetry and set me on the path to becoming a writer, even though at that age what I really wanted to be was an actress. She became my role model for what a teenage girl should be, and everything about her was in some way incorporated into my life. My bedroom became a facsimile of hers, and it was a place of refuge where I could write poetry or letters, read her cast-off copies of 'TEEN magazine, or listen to James Taylor, or Carly Simon, or Bread, the music she introduced me to.

She took me on the train into Geneva for magical afternoons when the world was just she and me, and anything was possible. We shopped in department stores like Grand Passage, where I bought my own bottles of peach-scented shampoo. We ate at upscale pizzerias like Vedia, or at imitation American hamburger restaurants like Wimpy's. I held her hand crossing the street and together we watched impossibly sophisticated men and women move like lacquered angels through the streets of this most glamorous international city of watches, jewelry and the tireless nurture of other peoples' fortunes. We walked and walked till the blue hour of early dusk, when the mist came in off Lake Geneva and the colors of the great floral clock near the train station grew moody and subdued in the dying light. At the water's edge, the seagulls swooped low over the city, long gray shadows in the brilliant electric rainbow footlights of Geneva's famous *jette d'eau,* the spectacular fountain that explodes out of the lake in an arc of liquid silver, shattering across the night water like a shower of emeralds, rubies, diamonds and sapphires. I was completely at peace in Nancy's safe, protective embrace, and whatever I was or wasn't didn't matter to either of us.

My mother appreciated that when Nancy was around, I was calmer and less prone to inexplicable fits of rage and lashing out. Nancy's mother worried that I was in love with her daughter. The thought that I wanted to be Nancy never occurred to either of them

Declaring Nancy my standard of beauty, I began to collect makeup of my own that I kept in a pretty wicker basket on my dresser—American beauty products like the blushing gel Nancy brought back from Cincinnati. I told my mother this was "stage makeup," for practising "my acting," and that I was determined to become a

127

THE LOVE THAT DARE NOT SPEAK ITS NAME

Master of Disguise using it. Generously, if inexplicably, my mother turned a blind eye to my predilection for cosmetics, and I practised applying them in private in the sanctuary of my bedroom. By thirteen, I was so skilled at painting my face that I could leave the house wearing blush and/or foundation, with no one (including my parents) any the wiser. I smoothed Nivea cream into my face every night before bed to keep my face smooth, as the fashion magazines urged.

Nancy's favorite perfume was Chantilly, a spicy, floral fragrance that I still associate with her even though she has long since stopped wearing it. She gave me her empty perfume bottles and powder-boxes, and they lined my dresser until I got the courage to buy my own bottle of Chantilly cologne to wear on weekends. In the same way I discovered that pink lipstick was almost undetectable if applied lightly, I learned that if cologne was sprayed in the air above my head in a mist, then walked through, the scent was light enough to be a mere suggestion of bouquet. My use of cosmetics had nothing to do with making myself look different or pretty; it had to do with taking part in a resolutely feminine ritual, something inflexibly forbidden to boys, a tangible gender barrier and one of the few I could vault. Applying makeup and scent near-invisibly was a powerful symbol. I could nurture the girl inside yet "pass" as a boy in the outside world. It was an affirmation of my femaleness that I hadn't previously had available. Like the place in my head I'd taken my dolls and my mother's clothes and jewelry to, the limitless landscape behind my eyes was the place I took these new symbols: a private place where I was simply what I was, and all was right with the world.

Nancy loved me, and I loved her. She gave me two precious gifts that I realize in retrospect likely saved me from suicide, something that began to occur to me regularly in my early teenage years when the storm inside me began to turn the skies of my adolescence black and cold and violent. Nancy was the first person to every love me unconditionally and nurture and celebrate everything about me, including the things that drew opprobrium from others like lightning. Furthermore, she was the first person in my life who allowed me to use her as a role model. She allowed me to project the fragmented pieces of my shattered and fragmented gender identity onto her, and in the light of her love and accept-

ESSAYS ON QUEER DESIRE AND SEXUALITY

ance I was able to see and assemble them into something I could live with.

The second seismic event in my life occurred one afternoon after gym class, and I remember it like it happened yesterday. In French, gym class was called *le sport*, as though the entire humiliating travesty of being the one no one wanted on the team was a healthy exercise in *mens sana in corpore sano*, as though being the weak one, the one the teacher made climb the rope while everyone else waited with derisive, sadistic impatience, was a jovial lesson in being a good sport, and if I didn't enjoy the fun and healthful *bonhomie* of a class that every other boy in the world looked forward to and thought of as his favorite, well, that was my problem, and another example of my maladaptive strangeness.

We had been playing soccer. The locker room was close and stuffy with the musk of pre-teen boys who hadn't quite made the transition between boyhood and young adulthood, for whom personal hygiene wasn't always a priority. I remember a cacophony of sound, the raucous, cracking laughter of boys, towels snapping, the gym teacher shouting at us to hurry up and get dressed or there would be hell to pay.

Suddenly, there was the sound of exploding glass, and the locker room was plunged into darkness. There was a moment of stunned silence then someone shouted, *What the fuck?* in French, and everyone started to babble. There was nervous laughter as boys fumbled in the darkness with their wet soccer clothes and gym bags. There was the sound of someone's head smacking into a metal locker, an expletive, then more laughter.

I had learned to love the darkness for the peace it represented, and I closed my eyes and savored it, standing still, knowing that any minute someone would replace the overhead bulb and the moment of silent evenness would end.

Two hands, strong hands, grasped the sides of my face in the darkness, insistent yet curiously gentle. I gasped as they pulled my face forward, and I was kissed, full and hard, on the mouth. The lips were full and slightly chapped, and I felt the warmth of a tongue tasting the inside of my mouth, and I tasted it back. The kiss grew more forceful. I tentatively reached out and touched two naked, muscular arms and the thick, soft, damp hair of a boy I couldn't see. I leaned forward in answering

129

THE LOVE THAT DARE NOT SPEAK ITS NAME

insistence, feeling a smooth hard chest brush against mine. As I pressed my own lips hard against those of my invisible lover, I felt something like my soul leaving my body, taking flight into the miraculous darkness.

Then I heard a regretful sigh and the lips left mine. The heat of the other boy's body retreated, and I was alone, flushed and wide-eyed in the blackness of the locker room.

I winced in the sudden cruel whiteness of the overhead light as it went back on.

Across the room, I saw the janitor descending the short stepladder he'd climbed to replace the bulb. Wildly, I looked around me, trying to see who was standing near enough to have been the one who kissed me, but all the boys seemed equidistant, and none of them were looking in my direction. No one was looking *away* from me either, but all the boys were fully engaged in what they were doing prior to the light going out: showering, snapping towels, getting dressed, zipping gym bags, hurrying out of the locker room.

Standing half-naked beside the locker, my body was alive with sensation, and I blushed to experience the unfamiliar fire in my chest, the damp flush of my cheeks, the hardness below the towel. I touched my mouth, feeling the ghost-imprint of that vividly male kiss burn my fingers, and I knew that nothing would ever be the same after that moment. Absolutely nothing.

I spent my teenage years at St. John's Cathedral Boy's School, a macho prep school on the prairies of western Manitoba. The school was intensely physical and rigorous, and was run by a lay branch of the Anglican Church of Canada. It was designed to promote what the Victorians called "muscular Christianity." My entry to the school was swift and brutal, but the mercy of it was the fact that once I was beaten up a couple of times for being "a faggot," I was accorded both space and distance to recoup my energies, and figure out a way to not only survive, but thrive.

To do so, I buried the world behind my eyes—and the girl who lived there—deep enough to render them both invisible.

I was a formidable wit and a punishing mimic, and in a cloistered

130

ESSAYS ON QUEER DESIRE AND SEXUALITY

environment like a boy's school, there is always room (and even grudg-
ing admiration) for someone tough enough to endure razzing, especially razzing of the cruelest kind. I made close friends over the next four
years, and made a name for myself as the school's writer and dramatist,
penning Christmas plays that skewered the teachers without sending up
any red flags. In my second year, I met Barney, a dazzling, handsome,
transfer student from Vancouver, and we became lovers. Barney's tenderness was like yarrow, drawing pain from me and offering a sense of
completeness in its stead. His passion and erotic skill, even at sixteen,
was extraordinary. We became fast friends as well as lovers. When the
curiosity about sex and the passion faded away, the friendship
remained.

Neither of us considered ourselves "gay," of course. Barney had a
girlfriend back in Vancouver, and I was in a sexual limbo. I didn't want
to be gay. The "ugliness" and "perversion" of homosexuality had been
pounded into me by age seventeen, and nothing positive about the
evolving gay culture of the late 1970s ever reached me through the bar-
ricade of unquestioned homophobia that bordered my world. I recoiled
at the photographs of moustachioed East Village clones I saw in *Time*
magazine, seeing only disorder and an alien world that was more scary
and lonely than the one I was in.

Even when Barney told me about gay porn he had seen, nothing in
the man-on-man sex struck me as attractive, erotic or relevant to my life.
On some secret, private level, I still saw a girl in the mirror. I was still
waiting to be *someone's girlfriend*, and that was the ideal. The knowledge
that I would never be that, that I likely was gay, was unbearable, and I
pushed it far down into my subconscious.

I was jealous of the girls my buddies picked up at the mall or the
roller rink. In their tight jeans and Farrah Fawcett hair, they seemed the
luckiest beings in creation. They had the power to turn the boys I lived
with twenty-four hours a day into men I didn't recognize. Men who
swaggered, who spoke in low, confident voices, who went to any lengths
to appear strong and masculine and dominant, and yet, at the same time,
danced attendance to these girls like pleasure slaves. I stood back in awe
on Sunday mornings and watched my roommates shave, apply flesh-
toned Clearasil, sculpt their hair with The Dry Look, and don clean jeans

THE LOVE THAT DARE NOT SPEAK ITS NAME

or cords, and crisp shirts, unbuttoned to expose chest hair. My own ablu-
tions took far less time, as all I was dressing for was the library, where I
would read fashion magazines, or the cinema where I watched horror
movies like *The Fury* and *Halloween*. I wasn't lonely, far from it. I regularly had invitations from school and family friends to spend the weekend with them, but there was much more peace and pleasure to be found
in retreating to the place behind my eyes where I had been living since I
was a child. Without my friends to reflect myself back to me the way
they saw me, I was free to be myself, in private.

Another window to the world opened the summer I was sixteen. I
signed with a model agency in my hometown of Ottawa, Ontario, and
began what was to be a successful, short career as a teenage male model.
The fact that modeling was considered a classically feminine career had
definite appeal. There was an irony in my working in a world of beauty,
makeup, bright lights and glamour while the stylists and the photogra-
phers turned me into the clean-cut all-American jock I knew I wasn't. I
was usually the youngest male model on the shoot, and the older female
models thought I was adorable as I quizzed them about their work, their
beauty routines and their lives. I memorized their stories, and hoarded
them like jewels. Every summer, I would return home to Ottawa, check
in with my agency and make the rounds with my portfolio. All summer,
I would shoot catalogues and magazine spreads in Ottawa and
Montreal, then return to St. John's in the fall to my "other life," and bide
my time till graduation.

After graduation, I packed up my portfolio and took off to Paris,
ostensibly to model, but mostly to try to make sense of my life. I was
nineteen, and my attraction to men had led me to the very logical conclusion that I was gay. I came out, embraced that identity and began living as a gay man. What little I knew of transsexuality was limited to
movie-of-the-week cliches and the thought of having an operation to
become a woman was beyond anything I could conceive of. I had, by
then, largely reconciled myself to the duality of my gender and sexual
nature. If I was two people—one male, one female—then so be it. I liked
them both. I had little knowledge of gay life, but I was convinced that in
this new world—free from the prying eyes and demands for accountability of friends and family—I would be allowed to be who I was with-

ESSAYS ON QUEER DESIRE AND SEXUALITY

out apology. All I asked of it was that it allow me to be the person I was inside, and allow me to find someone to love, who would in turn love me back.

I had sex with a man for the first time when I was in Paris—a man, not a boy—and there was none of the hurried rush and friction that had defined my prep-school encounters. I returned home from Paris in time for Christmas, came out to my oldest friend and moved to Toronto in the new year. There, I threw myself into the joy of my new freedom. I danced, I visited bathhouses, I dated, I had sex with anyone I wanted, and nearly everyone who wanted me. For the first time in my life I was able to hold men close, to be held. My dual gender wasn't an issue for once, and it blended together seamlessly. In 1982, I retired from modeling and entered the University of Toronto with the goal of becoming a writer. I fell in love several times, had my heart broken as many times as I fell in love. I published inert love poetry in campus literary journals and journalism that the editors of commercial magazines thought were excellent.

In 1984, at twenty-one, I left school to try to become a real writer. That summer, I met a young physician. He was kind and handsome, and had the most beautiful speaking voice I had ever heard. I fell irrevocably in love. Fortunately, he fell in love with me as irrevocably, and we moved in together. In 1985, we did something unusual for the times: we got married in a church. I told him about my life, about the woman in my head and heart who had been the defining architect of my inner world. Miraculously, he told me he understood. In loving me, he wasn't just looking *past* my history; he looked *through* it, seeing something beautiful there that I myself had never seen. Where I saw a shattered, fragmented psychosexual landscape, he saw a complex and beautiful one, gentle, tender and loving. He accepted me completely and utterly, and in doing so, freed me to be completely and utterly myself. For the first time, I felt an unfamiliar, exciting, masculine energy move in and take over. I was protected enough by my partner's acceptance of me *as I was* to taste my incumbent masculinity, explore it and eventually welcome it. There was a powerful allure to the alignment between body and mind, and I gradually came to understand that there had been a man there the whole time, slumbering for years, now stirring and stretching, asserting his

THE LOVE THAT DARE NOT SPEAK ITS NAME

rightful place, as though my body had only been a leasehold whose deed belonged to him.

The woman in my head still came and went as she pleased, but now her eyes were not the only eyes through which I saw the world. Some mornings I woke up and she was there, and she would select my frame of mind as though it were an outfit, discarding moods and perspectives with feminine caprice. Other mornings, I would wake feeling completely male and would assess her row of perfumes and skin creams on the bathroom vanity with something between disorientation and disdain. I loved the power of the man in my head, and longed to have him linger, but he never did. *She* always came back, and she treasured the prerogatives of her gender. Nothing was ever thrown away, and both of them lived inside me in an uneasy truce.

One night, I was working out at the YMCA in Toronto. At twenty-four, I was out of university and working a series of low-paying jobs while I concentrated on launching my career as a freelance magazine journalist. The pace was hectic, but I was young enough to handle it, and my time at the gym was a wonderful stress-reliever. I was proud of my body: my flat stomach, my runner's legs, the breadth of my shoulders and the strength of my arms. After lifting weights, I dove into the swimming pool and began to do laps. The water was cool and blue, and as it swept over my body, caressing my skin and cooling my flushed muscles, my thoughts began to swirl and surge, and my heart began to pound. Feeling the edge of panic, I swam to the pool deck to catch my breath and looked up.

A man in his mid-thirties, broad shouldered, hairy, with powerful arms and striated thighs, was doing stretches in preparation for his swim. His body was that of a rugby player, the sort of classic male body built for bursts of strength, brute force and endurance rather than decorative beauty. He wore pale blue nylon swim-shorts, functional, not fashionable or decorative, and when he bent, the thin fabric stretched across his powerful buttocks. His thick black hair was damp with sweat and his eyes were dark. His features were indelicate: strong nose, square jaw and a defiant chin. If I ever saw masculinity incarnate, it was at this moment. Even though it seems unlikely, given his distance from me, I felt I could *smell* him, and I swooned. What I was looking at was the

ESSAYS ON QUEER DESIRE AND SEXUALITY

embodiment of something completely alien to me: his indisputable maleness summoned an answering femaleness in me: a desire to be taken, invaded, filled up with his *oppositeness*. I craved it. It was something beyond the mere sexual attraction with which I was well versed. No, this was about archetypes, collision, perfect fit. If there was ever a moment when I felt completely female, it was then.

My body was the wrong body, and I believed that I would die if I remained in it.

He dove into the pool, and I swam several paces behind him, watching his strong body plow through the blue water. He swam with determination, and when he reached the opposite end of the pool, he executed a perfect flip, launching himself off the pool wall and rocketing towards me. As he passed, his leg brushed mine. Impossibly, I had a vivid impression of muscle and hair, physical strength that surpassed mine, and, it seemed rightfully so. I imagined him pressing into me, my own flesh yielding to take him in, the impact of our two opposite but complementary sexual realities. As I scissor-kicked, I felt a phantom smoothness between my legs. My own body felt satiny and light and delicate in the water, and I stretched languorously in the cool blue. I followed him for a few more laps then I climbed out of the pool, showered, got dressed and went home.

I told my partner that I needed to have a sex change, that I was physically not the person I was inside, and indeed never had been.

I asked him if he loved me, and he said yes. I asked him if he could love me as a woman. He held me, and told me that he would always love me and support me, but that he was a gay man, not a straight man, and if I changed my sex, I would be taking the man he was in love with and replacing a woman he would *love*, but not be *in love with*.

I wept bitterly, thinking of the few happy years I had spent as a fully-integrated gay man, the way I had finally located the male identity that had eluded me for most of my life. I treasured it. At that moment, I hated the woman in my head for this last imperious assault on my psyche.

I thought of my life, the way it was growing and evolving, and the gifts and yield I had already harvested from it. I thought of the long road to self-acceptance, the way I had begun to love myself, as I never could

THE LOVE THAT DARE NOT SPEAK ITS NAME

before. I thought of my partner, who was holding me with such assured strength.

I could claim all this as mine, once and for all, or I could change my body to suit the woman who lived in my head, in the place behind my eyes that was as real as anything I could touch, whose need to assert herself had become so real and so insistent, and begin again.

I told my partner I wished that I was dead. He held me and assured me of how glad he was that I was alive, how much more perfect the world was for my presence in it, and how much he loved me. I thought of the years I believed that love was the exclusive province of the born-blessed, a privilege that others took for granted, and one to which no one as damaged as I was should even dare to aspire. As he held me, I wept against his shoulder, soaking his shirt. I felt a great ripping somewhere deep in the depths of my soul, as though I was being torn in half.

The facts of my own personal physical history today are resolutely unremarkable. I am a forty-year-old gay man with dark brown hair and blue eyes. My skin is pale and burns before tanning in a way that is classically English. I've been called handsome, and I'm pleased to say that with the exception of smile crinkles around my eyes that I'm rather fond of (and which people tell me make me look friendly), I'm "aging well." I tend towards largeness, not necessarily in bodyweight, but in the sense of a certain muscular lack of physical delicacy—a breadth of shoulders, a length of stride, of height. I *occupy space* in a way that is archetypally male. I am like my father in many ways, and like him, I can be effortlessly dominant in a way that doesn't always serve me well. I dress conservatively in a way that suits me, I think. There is nothing remotely feminine in my appearance or delivery, and no one sees the woman who lived in my head when they look at me. Frankly, I don't see her any more myself, and I sometimes miss her. She was with me for many good years, and I knew her as well as I know myself now. She seems to me now like a beloved, long-dead relative who lives in the warm amber of memory.

I made the defining choice that night when I was twenty-four, and whatever my life could have been if I had altered its physical manifestation, it wouldn't have been better than the life I have now. Perhaps *as good*, but not *better*. My partner and I celebrated our eighteenth anniver-

136

ESSAYS ON QUEER DESIRE AND SEXUALITY

sary this year. His love is my bulwark, and both of us have allowed the each other to be the best he can be, and both of us are individuals. As I've said before, my day begins with the sight of his sleeping face on the pillow next to mine, and ends with the warmth of his body pressed next to mine in the dark, the sound of his soft breathing, his arm protectively thrown across my back. Our friends think of us as a model couple, let alone a model *gay* couple. I identify fully and joyously as a gay man, without apology and without ambivalence. I take pleasure in my body, in its strength and its hardness, its capacity to give and receive pleasure, its ability to endure pain when necessary and its potential to protect me and those I love. I savor the differences between men and women, and occasionally find myself guilty of enjoying the male prerogatives that society has deemed my birthright. I have found comfort and peace in the perfect *click* between the exterior and the interior in a way that I couldn't have dreamed of when I was a young man on the threshold of my own life.

In the summer of 2002, I met two special women, both of whom had been men a million years ago, though in the face of their seamless femininity I was unable to locate traces of it. They were both beautiful, both kind, both fiercely intelligent. Their strength was Promethean. I was in awe of it. Their life stories moved me beyond measure, and their accomplishment—aligning their bodies to suit their female gender—caused me to marvel. Through meeting them, I was finally able to confront my own most personal and private history, and I was able to write it for the first time. I would be proud to believe that had I taken their path, I would have managed it with as much grace as they have. They are women, and their transgender is a badge of courage. I respect them too much to claim that title myself. I can't bring myself to compare my ordeal to theirs. Whatever I am, or was, I elect to leave it unnamed, and I live in the present now.

At the same time, I dream of a day when any of us—lesbian, gay, transgendered or anything in between—can take our places fully in the wider society, without reference or apology. A world that encompasses and celebrates *true* difference and diversity strikes me as something worth dreaming of and working for. The notion that the things which make us truly different and special ought to be treasured is wonderful. I

THE LOVE THAT DARE NOT SPEAK ITS NAME

dream of that day's eventual arrival, and I pray that even if I'm not here to see it, some young person as plural as I was will be loved and allowed to live as he is, without pressure to be something he isn't and indeed could never be. My writing has enabled me to explore many facets of gay life, focusing on the intersection between gay and straight culture, and why it is so terribly, terribly important that we all learn to celebrate what makes us different and unique and perfect, instead of wielding such sharp chisels in the relentless, bloody drive towards conformity.

I sense her presence inside me on certain days, but they're rare. She's a lady, after all, and would never impose herself in any obdurate way.

I feel her tenderness when I comfort a crying child or a frightened dog. I feel a sense of proud, primal identification in the presence of certain women who embody the highest attainment of their gender, strong women who see no conflict between power and nurturing, women anyone would be proud to be. I feel her coquettish shade pass through me when I am in the company of a particularly handsome young man, or a twinge when I see a young mother whispering sweetness in the ear of her rapt infant or a grandmother surrounded by adoring grandchildren, content in the knowledge that she will leave this earth well-seeded, and that she will live on in the eyes of her descendants. I remember her history when I catch the odd scent of Chantilly perfume, or the cool evening dampness of lake mist that reminds me of Geneva on a rainy afternoon. In those vertiginous moments, I gather up the discordant facets of my character, anoint them, and call them beautiful. I thank her for that gift of special sight and call myself blessed.

Last January, I left my father's home in Victoria, and took the ferry back to Vancouver. I tucked the photographs away in my Filofax. I looked at them several times on the long ride. I stared and stared into the eyes of the little boy in the housedress and desperately tried to locate the line of demarcation between where he ceased to be and where the man I am today began.

I felt tears gather briefly as I looked into his sweet face, but I wiped them away lest anyone on the crowded ferry saw me and stared. Men rarely cry. Most of us have forgotten how. I learned that lesson, as well as many others, a long time ago.

A Sea of Decaying Kisses

JUSTIN CHIN

Anna May Wong is dead. Left on some ice float, lips unkissed. Anna May Wong and Mae West were the only two Hollywood leading ladies that never got to kiss their leading men. The studio brass thought that there was too much smoldering sexuality already without the smack of lip contact.

I used to date this Dutch man. The only thing I can remember about our time together is him saying, "Suck my tongue; suck it hard." I can't even remember his name, what he looked like, what his body or hair felt like in my hands. Nothing. Nothing but that voice—probably not even his, but someone else's that I've replaced in my memory—telling me how to kiss him.

I have a friend who believes that the truth of love lies in the act of tongues. He refuses to kiss anyone unless he's positively sure that he's in love with that person. Once he's sure, he'd rather deep kiss than indulge in any fondling or anything ejaculatory. Once they kiss, once those lips touch, tongues slipped into the others' mouth, *Wham!* That's it, he wants the person to be his forever.

Aren't you placing an inordinate power in a tongue? I once asked him. An act? An organ that ceases to work if you can't smell, if your nasal passages are blocked by allergies or bad sinuses? But he doesn't hear me, as he's busy thinking about someone he kissed four weeks ago. I hate to admit it, but sometimes I think he's right. When you kiss someone, it's the first taste of his mouth that will make or break your heart.

Acupuncturists believe that you can tell what ails the body by looking at the tongue. The coating of the tongue, how the tissue looks, how it hangs in your mouth, the cracks, the shape, how wet it is. Everything about the tongue all points to something in your body. Every part of your body has

THE LOVE THAT DARE NOT SPEAK ITS NAME

some casual connection with your tongue.

I'm on the plane looking at the man beside me. I'm looking at his hands. Big, rough. There's some downy black hair on the back of his hands, on the flesh of the back of the fingers. He picks up the small airline muffin from his food tray, cuts it into thirds with the plastic knife, smears some spread on it and brings it to his partner's mouth. He holds the piece between his thumb and middle finger, the second finger outstretched, ready to wipe the bit of crumb and butter off the side of his partner's lips. I stare at his hands through the whole trip. Two rings: a wedding band and a collegiate-looking pinkie ring, chunky with fake green gemstones looking like moss on gold. Hands, fingers to mouth, tongue. Along with a good smooch, I want a slice of tenderness.

"My love life (underline) (period) My love life is sometimes good (comma) sometimes bad (period) When it is good (comma) I am happy (period) When it is bad (comma) I feel sad (period)"

Inevitably, I find myself hanging out at Cafe Loveless, home of broken queer hearts. Warm coffee, warm soy milk and warm draft beer, first refills free. The fridge broke down in 1986; the Half-&-Half ran out three years ago and never got replaced. You get to choose your coffee: Bitter Black or Diabetic Shock. Don't bother asking for an ashtray, there aren't any. Just tip your cigarette over the edge of the table; flick your ashes to the floor. Use your shoe to wipe it into the ground. You can request tango music. Just ask the man behind the bar, but nobody feels like dancing much at Cafe Loveless. Just want to sit on the hard plastic chairs and nurse a warm coffee or warm beer, ashes underfoot, wanting to lick the spill off someone's fingertips. All dreaming of hot Fabio-like romance while the jukebox racks up the compact disc of Linda Ronstadt's greatest hits. *That'll be the day, when you say goodbye, that'll be the day* . . . .

It's been so long since I've been in love with someone that is in love with me in return that I can't imagine the knowledge of knowing someone's body so intimately. How you can both be lying naked together on some lazy afternoon and you know where the soft and ticklish spots on the other body are, where the hard unfeeling parts crusted with dry dead

140

ESSAYS ON QUEER DESIRE AND SEXUALITY

skin are, where the hair is thick and luxurious, where it is soft and where it is a scant fuzz.

These days I'm only left to obsess about men that I chance across. An obsession is different from being smitten. One, you want to know every detail about the prey; the other, you just want to fill in the blanks with your fancy.

I'm trying to figure out what it is about this man that obsesses me. What it is that makes me think of him all the time, want to hear his voice, imagine him standing outside my door.

I love the way he moves: how his whole body, compact and sinewy, cuts through the air, determined and hard. I love his body hair: the way the stray strands of chest hair carelessly wisp out of the top of his T-shirt and curl in the hollow of his neck; how the hairs on his forearms mat down out of his rolled up shirt sleeves, looking soft and shivery. I love the way he holds his cigarette even though I am an avid non-smoker, and I love the smell of stale cigarette smoke on his clothes. I love his tattoos. I love the way his ears feel. I love the way he leaves the smell of his body on my body, the taste of his tongue in my mouth.

Once, I fell in love with an architect simply because I loved the fact that he makes buildings. Great big buildings. That such a small man made great structures out of steel and concrete that hold people and things up, pull them away from the ground and hold them up to the scrutiny of air, gravity and the elements.

I'm at the premiere of a really bad play that I co-wrote. It's another one of those funny coincidences that there are all these men that I have had affairs with, there with their little non-threatening boyfriends in tow. Well, I really wasn't having an affair with them; they were having an affair with me, which is a small but significant difference. At any rate, they were all trying to ignore me or else be very cordial and brief with me. Something about boyfriend being jealous, something about protecting their happy home lives: the whole idea of the two-bedroom-apartment-one-joint-vacation-a-year-let's-cook-together-darling lives. The red-light special at Relationships R Us, open 24 hours, 365 days a year.

141

THE LOVE THAT DARE NOT SPEAK ITS NAME

During the intermission, I think all their avoidance and their nerv-
ousness that I might say or do something to ruin their domestic bliss is
quite funny. By the end of the play—and it is more dreadful than I
thought it would be—I began to see the pathetic nature of the whole set-
up.

Jealousy. They want to avoid the bugbear of jealousy.

I'm sitting at a cafe when a man, whom I once had sex with while
he and his boyfriend were in the middle of yet another of their never-
ending undefined breakups, joins me. I haven't seen him in yonks and
we chat a little, suggestions of a future tryst. He can't sit too long,
boyfriend (they made up, apparently) may see us, he says. *Jealousy.*

"I thought you two had an open relationship," I say. His words are
"modern relationship," or "modern couple," or something equally nau-
seatingly vague. "Doesn't matter, he'll still get jealous," he tells me.

You only get jealous because you want to be all things to the person
you're smitten by or you think you're smitten by. Doesn't matter if you're
not that thing or don't ever want to be that thing; you just want your
sweetie to think that you are. And that's when you end up wearing stupid little tank tops and little cut-off shorts simply because your sweetie
found some tramp attractive in them, never mind you look like some
twitting idiot outside of your regular T-shirt and jeans ensemble that he
first fell in love with you in. It's worse when it's not something physical
like clothes or hair or body. Suddenly, you find yourself laughing different, moving different, method acting. Yikes. The superior ones simply
smack their sweeties on the head and develop an intense hatred towards
their sweeties' obsessions. The inferior ones crumble.

Jealousy. All it takes is one chaste smooch to betray.

I used to date a man who was obsessed with the color of the water in his
toilet bowl. Blue. He wanted it to be as blue as possible. To achieve this,
he resorted to dumping two or three of those blue-dying toilet bowl
cleansers into the cistern every week. Once, he even used dye, but that
only stained the porcelain.

It really got to be an obsession. When he entered his house, the first
thing he did was head straight for the bathroom and flush the bowl. He
even brought the blue cleanser tablets when he went on a trip, just in

case the hotel's toilet bowl didn't flush blue. Several times every night, he disentangled himself from our legs, arms and the twisted sheets to go and flush the toilet.

All this was fine, but I guess I knew the relationship wouldn't work out because I liked to piss in the bowl and watch the blue water turn green then yellow. I derived the same childish satisfaction as I did in all those years of high school chemistry laboratory, where I delighted in watching the liquids in the test tubes gradually precipitate and change colors in a glorious chemical reaction. Suddenly, the most boring white powders would turn into a stunning cloudy crimson, or the bland milky liquid would hiss and spit gas and turn into a silver suspension floating in a thick greenish-yellow solution. Of course, I was supposed to be observing how the periodic table and the elements and compounds that make up this world we live in affect our lives, but damn, those colors!

Years later, I happened to see him on public access television. He had his own show about psychic powers. Come to think of it, he always did say he was psychic. He was talking about spirit guides, those proverbial "little voices in your head," and how they talked to you. He asked the viewers to ask their spirit guides to tell them what color he was thinking of in his head. I guessed blue. I was right.

Seeing him on that program and knowing that he was psychic made me feel so much better. At least now I know he knew that I wasn't going to return his phone calls. Still, in spite of his bizarre obsessions, he was really a rather sweet person. And he's also the first man out of many that I wish I had kissed goodbye properly.

Then there was this other guy. Every time he got aroused, his salivary glands kicked in and he would salivate like mad. This meant he always had to spit. He kept a little spittoon (it was a cheap waste basket, really) with tissues wadded on the bottom beside his bed for this purpose. You would think it was quite gross, but actually he was a damn good kisser.

I knew a man I was dating was far too sensitive for me when he locked himself in the bathroom after I came home with various of my body parts pierced.

"Oh honey," he said through the locked door, his voice some kind of whimpering sob. "Piercing your body! But why? It's . . . it's such a random act of violence."

"Well, sweetie," I tried reasoning with him after I lured him out of the loo by lying about needing to shit real bad because of bad bacon. "It's hardly random. It's not like I was caught in a drive-by piercing."

Conventional wisdom has it that the most sensitive people are the best smoochers. This man was a horrid kisser, actually: too much teeth, too little tongue and too much force. In this case, conventional wisdom and Newton's Second Law of equal opposite reactions seemed to have betrayed me.

I'm trying to remember my first kiss but I can't.

Obsessions are best kept that way. It's really not wise to try and bring them to you even if you desperately want to. Even if you're horny beyond belief.

I discovered this with another obsession of mine. I met him quite by chance — the best way to meet anyone. For a week after our meeting, I kept saying his name over and over because I liked the way the syllables bumped into each other in my mind.

He works for a large chemical corporation, but tells people that he is a photographer and a video maker. He likes horror fiction, were-wolves and vampires, that sort of thing. He writes short fiction and is on a gothic horror kick: Asylum doctor turns into an insect in a despicable plot by alien spiders trying to breed flies out of humans for consumption. He wants to take my picture, he tells me as we wait for the J-Church. He says I will end up looking Japanese when the picture comes out. I say no. He begs, says, "Please, please, I'll do anything, anything." I tell him no. "I don't like cameras," I say. He walks to the edge of the platform, turns around and says, "Anything" one more time. He tells me how great the picture will look: half my face in shadows, half in a blinding light.

He gives me some of his writing to read. I wish he hadn't. I am not shocked by the writing at all. The improbability of it all does nothing to scare me. I tell him about Oliver Sacks' work, about how people are trapped for years inside a dead lifeless body, active minds stuck in a life-

ESSAYS ON QUEER DESIRE AND SEXUALITY

less body, senses forced to watch everything change around them but powerless to feel or do anything. That's what scares me. He's unfamiliar with what I'm talking about. He gives me another piece. "It's unfinished," he says. "Help me find an ending."

Still, I love the way he says, "I've got a brilliant idea" when something strikes his mind. I like the way I sound like him when I'm reading an unfamiliar text out loud. He's making a video about werewolves. On the streetcar, he touches my chin, rubs the unshaven bits of fuzz and asks me if that was intentional. I say it's not. I rub his scant goatee, too, and he laughs. He tells me that he just recently had to change his aftershave, something about allergies causing blotches, and I remember the smell of his aftershave days ago when I leaned in to hug him goodbye. The smell of his aftershave mixed with the grimy smell of a workday. I get off the streetcar, cross the road, try not to look at him, but as the streetcar speeds by I see him through the plate glass of the back door. He's sitting with his legs up on the seat.

One night, I want to take him to Dolores Park. I want to sit him down in the middle of the park and I want to kiss him while the bats in the park are squealing because of the cold. Few people know that there are bats living in Dolores Park. I've lived around the park for two years. I didn't know myself. One day, I was walking past the park late at night to go to his place to pick up some papers and I heard the distinctive squeal of bats. Bats usually don't scream like that, the reference book in the library says. It must be the cold; they must be suffering.

One day I invite him over. We end up in my bedroom where we start fooling around. It all would have been fine if I wasn't so conscious of the fact that I had carefully folded his manuscript of writing that he had given me to read into neat kindling and laid the entire script of 30-odd pages in my fireplace. The unburnt manuscript-kindling resting under the packed-woodchip log just hidden from his view by the dark fireplace screen and my house guest periodically knocking on my door asking if I wanted a bacon and egg on white bread sandwich made the entire tryst quite unsettling. That, and his deformed left nipple.

As sexually liberated as I try to be, deformed nipples scare the shit out of me. I don't mind the severely pierced keloided ones because I know

145

they were manipulated into such a state; but the ones that slant off to strange tangents all by themselves, aureoles that cave into dark nipples that look like large blackheads, give me the heebie-jeebies.

Penises are a different matter though. I quite enjoy deformed penises. This is probably because the first penises that I was attracted to and spent hours staring at and masturbating to were those in my fathers medical books that he stored under my brother's bed.

Following the page numbers in the index, I was led to little shriveled diseased penises rotting through to the urethra, hanging bulbous members bloated to look like a fleshy tennis ball and dangling members in semi-erection to show the world its horrible scabs and sores—all found in fabulous color.

Perhaps this prepared me for the first pierced penis that I ever saw. It was at a jack-off party and somehow, it didn't faze me; in fact, I found it quite erotic, and I thought it was a shame the bugger it was attached to was more interested in wanking-off with someone else all evening. My companion, however, found the pierced dick quite unsettling and his balls immediately retracted into his body and he had to escape to the kitchen to recompose himself.

He later told me that he was unable to have a full erection for days after witnessing that penis.

Once, I had phone sex with a man. He had a very normal voice. Nothing exceptional. Tonal quality, inflection, phrasing—the kind of voice you hear on the street as you pass by two people chatting away or when the phone rings and it's someone you don't know, then gives you a name you don't remember and then tries to sell you investment information.

He wanted to be fucked in the arse without a condom, wanted to feel it: *been so long, man, really need to feel that hot cock in me.* I made him shoot his first load on my dick, then fucked him up his arse using his jism as lubricant. After I came, I put my hand under his arse, palm up and he squeezed the collective cum and anal mucus out of his rectum noiselessly onto my waiting palm then jacked off another load into my hand. He used his tongue to mix the two, his watery jism and my denser congealed jism into a swirl and licked it off my hand, every single drop. When that was done, I wiped my hand on his face, pulled him to me and kissed him hard on the mouth sucking his tongue roughly.

I'm trying to remember my first good kiss but I can't.

I've had incredibly bad luck with demonic-looking men. Sure, I find them vastly attractive, but somehow they seem to be attracted to other demonic-looking men. I try to look demonic but it really doesn't work with me. The best I can do is look like the boy next door's younger brother who lives beside the most gorgeous demonic-looking bloke.

The most erotic thing I have ever seen was this brilliantly demonic-looking man eating sushi with a metal fork. On anyone else, the sight would have been quite ridiculous, but on this one man, it was enough to make me want to cook him breakfast for the rest of my life.

In my search for a demonic-looking lover, I tried placing a classified ad in the local news weekly, but due to a typo, I was surprised to discover that there was quite a sizable number of actual Satanists in San Francisco.

The other day, as I was walking down the street, I discovered a new fetish: men with tattoos on the back of their necks. The back of a man's neck has always been the favorite part of man's body for me. This does get quite problematic, as I will often find myself getting quite aroused when I'm sitting behind a particularly sinewy neck on the bus or when the lights from the cinema screen hits the side of a fuzzed neck in front of me.

Ah! The cinema. At a re-screening of Bertolucci's filmic recreation of Bowles' *The Sheltering Sky,* I participated in some heavy flirtation with a man. Throughout the movie, I gave up on Debra Winger's search for her sexual self for that man's neck and how it glowed in the flickering of the screen. After the screening, I was determined to try to pick him up. I tried to approach him but the crowds cut me off, and when I did reach the foyer all that was left of him was the tub of popcorn he was munching into and the Dixie cup of soda resting in the empty popcorn tub: one in the other resting on the edge of the trash bin. Suddenly I was gripped with the urge to grab his trash and lick the tip of the straw where his lips lingered during John Malkovich's tragic and pointless death. Fortunately, the cinema manager came by and tipped the cartons into

THE LOVE THAT DARE NOT SPEAK ITS NAME

the bin and stomped the trash down with his boot to flatten it, thus saving me from embarrassing myself from such indecently obsessive acts.

Now I find myself falling behind men on the street who have black squiggles peeking out the tops of the back of their shirts. And worse, I find myself longing to lean over and place my lips on it. Nothing else but lip to neck.

The act of kissing a person's neck is possibly the most sensual act known to humankind. The neck is the body's most vulnerable spot: muscle, nerves and veins built around a vertebral column. In the animal kingdom, the smart mammals have been known to protect their necks vehemently; they never ever expose their necks unnecessarily. If you watch documentaries on hunters and the hunted—that's where lions bite deer and where lions bite each other. Never mind the little bit of flesh over the heart, there are ribs that protect it, but the neck—nothing.

The lips also are highly sensitive: something about all those blood vessels flowing so close to the surface and the close proximity to the tongue and all of its glands and sensory stuffs.

There is a proper way to kiss someone on the neck. First, you must always start on the back or the side. Second, and this is the most important thing, you must never, never touch the other person with any other part of your body. Only lip to neck, nothing else. Let the neck feel only the press of warm lips and the lips feel the vast flesh of neck. When this happens, the microscopic space between lip and neck heats up vastly because air is a poor conductor of heat. It's kind of like how a blanket or an animal fluffing its fur works. You may be in the middle of the Sahara and you will still feel that one intense spot of heat surging out of your lover's lips and through your neck.

Smooch music: Sam Cooke, Marvin Gaye, the Supremes, Dusty in Memphis, Ella doing Gershwin, Ella with Ellington.

It's late and I can't sleep. It's been raining like mad and the roof is leaking everywhere. Drops of water sneak down the fireplace and drop like flies on the dead ashes. I have to keep my curtains drawn to trap the heat. That's fine, but when the wind blows, the leaves and branches of the palm tree outside my window scrape against the pane. It makes a hideous sound. I know if I can see the smack of the frond on the pane,

148

it'll all be okay. But the curtains are drawn and I'm lying under three blankets and a sleeping bag trying not to move or I'll wake the damn cat curled up at the foot of the bed. I'm still trying to remember that first good kiss and the last good kiss and what happened in between, while Ella scats something fierce; and while my heart breaks again, Anna May Wong and Mae West are off somewhere holding each other's faces in their hands, teaching each other how to kiss.

Contributors

Patrick Califia is a bisexual, transgendered man who is also a prolific author, therapist and parent. On the far side of his forties, he is a long-time social critic, feminist and rabble-rouser. The many facets of sexuality (pleasure, gender, deviance and social control) have preoccupied him personally and professionally for most of his adult life. The second edition of *Public Sex*, a collection of his essays, has now been joined by another compendium, *Speaking Sex to Power*. He is currently working on a book about growing up queer in a blue-collar Mormon family.

Justin Chin is the author of *Burden of Ashes, Harmless Medicine, Mongrel: Essays, Diatribes and Pranks* and *Bite Hard*. His writings have appeared in *American Poetry: The Next Generation, The Outlaw Bible of American Poetry, The World in Us: Lesbian and Gay Poetry of the Next Wave* and *Chick for a Day*. He has created eight, full-length solo performance works and several shorter works that have been presented nationally and abroad. He has performed his work at PS 122 and Dixon Place in New York; Josie's Cabaret & Juice Joint, the LAB, Center for the Arts, Artist Television Access, Luna Sea & Southern Exposure in San Francisco; East/West Players in Los Angeles; the Cleveland Performance Art Festival, Hampshire College and Loyola University. Born in Malaysia and raised in Singapore, he currently lives in San Francisco.

Writer, filmmaker, director, and drag queen extraordinaire, **Sky Gilbert**, is one of North America's most controversial artistic forces. Founding artistic director of Buddies in Bad Times Theatre from 1979-1997, his Dora Award winning plays have been presented worldwide. ECW Press published his collection of poetry *Digressions of a Naked Party Girl* in 1998, and his theatre memoir *Ejaculations from the Charm Factory* in 2000. His first three novels: *Guilty* (1998), *St. Stephen's* (1999), and *I Am Kasper Klotz* (2001) were critically acclaimed. He is presently working on his fourth novel (to be published by Cormorant in 2003) and his Ph.D. at The University of Toronto. He also writes a weekly column for *Eye* magazine.

Francisco Ibáñez-Carrasco was born in Santiago de Chile and migrated to Vancouver, B.C. in 1985, where he acquired his HIV in 1986, his Canadian citizenship in 1991, his doctorate in Education from Simon Fraser University in 1999, and a long drawn appetite for writing. His short stories have been included in *Contra/Diction* (Arsenal Pulp Press, 1998), *Best Gay Erotica 2000* (Cleis Press), *Of the Flesh* (Suspect Thoughts Press, 2001), and *The Mammoth Book of Best New Erotica* (Carol and Graff Publishers, 2001) and on-line magazines such as *SuspectThoughts.com* and *VelvetMafia.com* (2002). His first novel, *Flesh Wounds and Purple Flowers: The Cha-Cha Years,* was published by Arsenal Pulp Press in 2001 and nominated for the Regional Commonwealth Prize in 2002. He freelances as social scientific researcher and university instructor in Vancouver, B.C. and serves volunteer time as Co-Chair of the Canadian Working Group on HIV and Rehabilitation. *Underbelly Tales,* a collection of his short fiction will be released in 2004 (Suspect Thoughts Press).

Marshall Moore escaped from North Carolina in 1994 and now leads a happy, stable and uneventful life in the San Francisco Bay Area, where the humidity is low, the cost of living is high and his closest living relative is thousands of miles away. His debut novel, *The Concrete Sky*, is forthcoming from Southern Tier Editions (Haworth Press).

Felice Picano's first book was a finalist for the PEN/Hemingway Award. Since then he has published twenty volumes of fiction, poetry, non-fiction and memoirs. Considered a founder of modern gay literature along with the other members of the Violet Quill Club, Picano also founded two publishing companies: the SeaHorse Press and Gay Presses of New York. Among his many award-winning books are the novels, *Like People in History* and *The Book of Lies.* His most recent novel, *Onyx*, was published to acclaim in 2001. Picano's exhibit "Early Gay Presses of New York," debuted at the ONE Institute in L.A. and will tour the country. San Francisco's New Conservatory Theatre will premiere Picano's new comedy-thriller, *The Bombay Trunk.*

Andy Quan has been an activist and writer since the late eighties, studying and working in gay rights and HIV/AIDS, and talking about sex, cultural diversity within queer communities and more. His fiction and poetry have appeared in many anthologies and magazines in North America, Europe and Australia including many appearances in the *Best Gay Erotica* series. Born in Vancouver, he now works in Sydney, Australia. He is the author of a book of poetry, *Slant*, and the Lambda Literary Award-nominated short fiction collection, *Calendar Boy*, which has been published in both North America and Australia.

Michael Rowe is the Lambda Literary Award-nominated editor of the anthologies *Queer Fear* and *Queer Fear II*, and the co-editor of two original vampire anthologies, *Sons of Darkness* and *Brothers of the Night*. An award-winning journalist and essayist whose work has appeared in *The National Post, The Globe and Mail* and *The Next City*, Rowe is the author of two critically acclaimed works of non-fiction, *Looking For Brothers* and *Writing Below The Belt*. A lifelong aficionado of the horror genre, his essays, articles and reviews have appeared in *The Scream Factory, Rue Morgue, All Hallows* and *Fangoria*. A member of both PEN Canada and The Horror Writers Association, he lives in Toronto with his life-partner, Brian McDermid.

Simon Sheppard is the author of *Hotter Than Hell and Other Stories* and the forthcoming non-fiction book *Kinkorama*. He's also the co-editor, with M. Christian, of the best-selling book *Rough Stuff* and its sequel, *Roughed Up: More Tales of Gay Men, Sex, and Power*. His work has appeared in all but one edition of *Best Gay Erotica*, three editions of *The Best American Erotica*, four of *Friction: Best Gay Erotic Fiction* and over 60 other anthologies, a number of which have "Best" in their titles, too. His second short story collection, *In Deep*, will be published by Alyson Books in 2004.

Michael V. Smith, an MFA grad from the University of British Columbia, was selected as one of Vancouver's Most Dangerous People by *Loop Magazine* in 2001. He produces the public sex 'zine *Cruising*, performs stand-up improv audience-participation nudist drag as Miss Cookie LaWhore and has made a number of tranny prostitution videos with filmmaker Nickolaos Stagias which toured film festivals across North America. Cormorant Books in Canada published his first novel,

Cumberland, to glowing reviews in the spring of 2002.

Matt Bernstein Sycamore is the author of the novel *Pulling Taffy* (Suspect Thoughts Press, 2003), and editor of the anthologies *Tricks and Treats: Sex Workers Write About Their Clients* (Haworth, 2000) and *Dangerous Families: Queer Writing Beyond Recovery* (Haworth, 2003). His writing has appeared in *The Best American Erotica 2001, Best American Gay Fiction 3, Best Gay Erotica 2000, 2001 and 2002, Blithe House Quarterly* and numerous other publications.

Royston Tester grew up in Birmingham, England. Before moving to Canada in 1979, he lived in Barcelona and Melbourne. His work has appeared in *Rip-Rap* and *Intersections* (Banff Centre Press), *Quickies 2* (Arsenal Pulp Press), *The Church-Wellesley Review, Descant, The Antigonish Review, PRISM International, Malahat Review, New Quarterly, Quarry, B&A New Writing* and *Queen Street Quarterly*. Tester has a Ph.D. in Modern British Literature. His first novel, *Nancy's Boy*, and first short fiction collection, *Hands Over The Body*, are currently doing the publishers' rounds through trail-blazing literary agent Anne McDermid. He lives in Toronto.

Emanuel Xavier is author of the self-published debut collection, *Pier Queen* (Pier Queen Productions, 1997), the Lambda Literary Award-nominated novel, *Christ-Like* (Painted Leaf Press, 1999) and the poetry collection, *Americano* (Suspect Thoughts Press, 2002). He is winner of a Marsha A. Gomez Cultural Heritage Award for his contributions to gay and Latino culture and lives in New York City.

About the Editor

Greg Wharton is the publisher of Suspect Thoughts Press, and the editor of two web magazines, *SuspectThoughts.com* and *VelvetMafia.com* (with Sean Meriwether). He is also the editor of the anthologies *The Best of the Best Meat Erotica* (Suspect Thoughts Press, 2002), *Law of Desire: Tales of Gay Male Lust and Obsession* (with Ian Philips, Alyson Books, 2004), *Love Under Foot: An Erotic Celebration of Feet* (with M. Christian, Southern Tier Editions-Haworth Press, 2004), and *Of the Flesh: Dangerous New Fiction* (Suspect Thoughts Press, 2001). *Johnny Was: and Other Tall Tales,* a collection of Wharton's short fiction will be released in 2003 (Suspect Thoughts Press).